Choosing a Better Life

Inspiring informative books for thoughtful readers wanting to develop themselves and realise their potential.

Other titles in the series include:

Picking Winners
*A total hiring system for spotting exceptional performers
and getting them on board*

Getting Your Next Job
*A systematic approach to find the career
that is best for you*

Healing the Hurt Within
*Understand and relieve the suffering
behind self-destructive behaviour*

Please send for a free copy of the catalogue for full details
(see back cover for address).

Choosing a
Better Life

An inspiring step-by-step guide to building the future you want

Hilary Jones and Frank Gilbert

PATHWAYS

First published in 1999 by
How To Books Ltd, 3 Newtec Place,
Magdalen Road, Oxford OX4 1RE, United Kingdom
Tel: 01865 798306 Fax: 01865 248780

British Library Cataloguing in Publication Data
A catalogue record for this book is available from
the British Library

Editing by David Venner / Cover image PhotoDisc
Cover design by Shireen Nathoo Design

Produced for How To Books by Deer Park Productions
Typeset by PDQ Typesetting, Stoke-on-Trent, Staffs.
Printed and bound in Great Britain

Note: The material contained in this book is set out in good
faith for general guidance and no liability can be accepted for
loss or expenses incurred as a result of relying in particular
circumstances on statements made in the book. The laws and
regulations are complex and liable to change, and readers
should check the current position with the relevant
authorities before making personal arrangements.

Pathways is an imprint of
How To Books

Contents

List of Illustrations

Preface

You may be wondering why you should read this book in preference to any other book about personal development, so let's begin by looking at just *some* of the things it can help you to achieve:

At work

◆ Satisfaction and enjoyment in your work, and as a result a high level of motivation and low (or no) stress.

◆ An understanding of the impact you have on people and how to use this to your benefit.

◆ Self-confidence and assertiveness.

◆ A positive influence on the people you work with or for – at all levels.

◆ A clear focus on what you want to achieve, both short term and long term.

At home

◆ Quality time spent with the people who mean the most to you.

◆ Time to enjoy yourself – relaxing or pursuing a hobby.

◆ An understanding of how to make the most of your relationships with other people.

◆ Reduced or no stress.

◆ A plan for the future that you really want.

You may feel that you have already achieved some of these things, and if you have that's great! Whether you have or not, ask yourself this question. Are you happy with your life as it is at the moment? *Really* happy, 100% happy – all of the time not just *some* of the time?

If the answer to the question is *no* or *sometimes* or anything other than an unqualified *yes*, then this book is for you and, by following it through, you stand to gain an enormous amount of pleasure from the end result – the *you* that you want to be.

How do we know this? Because we have spent over 15 years researching and continually developing the processes we describe in this book. We have run many successful training courses and conducted hundreds of one-to-one personal development coaching sessions based on these techniques. By putting our knowledge and experience into writing, we hope you too will be able to reap the rewards of choosing a better life.

We have worked with many people over the years who have already proved that the process you are about to go through can succeed. They have said it changed their lives for the better – and consequently the lives of some of the people around them. People who were previously very unhappy at work have followed the recommendations in this book and have been able to improve their quality of life by adjusting the balance between home and work. Some spend fewer hours at work, but those hours are far more enjoyable and productive. As a consequence they are more relaxed at home, which has improved their home life too.

This book follows the learning sequence we have used so successfully on our courses and in our coaching sessions. First, it encourages you to focus on what you really and truly want out of life and then looks at what you have actually got at the moment. For most people there is an imbalance. Often they are spending far more hours at work than they would like and consequently they are stressed and tired when they get home, which has a knock-on effect on the quality of their home life.

Second, it helps you peel back the layers and look at the *real* you: examining the things you do – consciously or subconsciously – that can prevent you from having what you want. This may be lack of confidence, being too submissive or being too aggressive. Whatever it is, once you have acknowledged and understood it you can begin to do something about it. Chapter by chapter this book will help you to overcome whatever is holding you back. By the time you get to the final chapter you will have all the information you need to help you build a better life.

To gain the most that you can from this book it is best to take it one step at a time. There are a number of exercises to do, all of which are designed to help you focus on important issues. Some may seem quick and easy, others harder and more time-consuming. But they all have a part to play and *each* exercise is an important step in building a better future. So try to resist the temptation to skip any. It would be useful to keep a special notebook to record your responses.

You *can* achieve the balance that is right for *your* life and enjoy the success and happiness that goes with it if you are willing to put in the effort to get there. You will find that you get out of this book what you put into it, you can constantly refer to it when you need help or guidance.

A number of case studies appear throughout the book. Each of these is based on actual people – all we have changed is their names.

We have used the male pronouns generally throughout the book. This is purely for ease of reading – no sexism is intended.

We sincerely hope that you enjoy this book and that it helps you to have a better life.

We would like to thank the following people for all their help, support and encouragement – we couldn't have done it without them. First, many thanks to all the people we have worked with over the years, whose desires to have better lives were the inspiration for this book. A very special thanks to Peter Crossland, Peter Holmes, Graham Johnson, Fiona Marlow and Elaine Wood, who read the early drafts of the book and gave us their constructive feedback. Thanks also to Giles Lewis and Nikki Read at How To Books, and our agent Charlotte Howard, for their belief and encouragement.

Last but not least, thanks to our families for believing in us: Rose, Kate and Tom Gilbert, and Bob Jones.

Hilary Jones and Frank Gilbert

CHAPTER 1

Who Am I? Where Am I?

T hink about a time in your life when you were very happy. It might be a particular time in your childhood, your teenage years, your years at university, getting married, having a child, a special holiday, a big achievement, a new job... something that stands out in your memory as bringing you great happiness. Try to remember how wonderful you felt. Close your eyes for a while and re-live that time over again, remembering the people, the scenery, the colours, the smells, the sounds, the tastes, the words, the feelings.

Feels good, doesn't it? Just by remembering and reliving that moment you should be able to recapture some of that happiness. Wouldn't it be wonderful if you could bottle it and keep it with you always?

As you journey through this book you will learn how happiness *can* be yours, day in and day out. Not necessarily constant euphoria, but an enjoyment of life that brings you contentment and satisfaction – a permanent 'feel-good' factor.

How much effort will it take to choose a better life?

There may be a price you have to pay – for example, changing your job, ending a relationship, altering the way you behave – and only *you* know whether you are prepared to pay it. But don't let that put you off because deciding whether or not you want to pay the price is part of the process of choosing a better life.

How long will it take you to build a new future? That's really up to you. This book will simply give you the tools that you need to do it. Look at it this way – how old are you? Suppose that you are 32 years old now and nowhere near where you want to be: in other words it has taken you 32 years to get to where you *don't* want to be! Putting this into perspective, it is likely to take a few months or years to get to where you *do* want to be. It won't normally happen overnight.

Before you can begin to think about being happier and more fulfilled you need to take some time to clarify where you are now and what it is that you really want out of your life. Many people have only a vague idea of what they want 'I'd like to be successful', or they worry or complain about what they *haven't* got or *haven't* done 'I can never find the time or the money to have a decent holiday'. Vagueness and negative thinking will not help anyone to achieve what they want.

Amongst other things, the first chapter will help you to examine your motivations for buying this book. You will find that you derive much more satisfaction from it if you know what you want the book to do for you.

So, let's begin! In this chapter you will be getting in touch with the real you: who you are, what motivates you, what you want out of life. To do this you need to answer a number of questions:

What do you hope to get out of this book?

When answering this question, think of it as the first stage on your journey to the life you want. This type of journey is more purposeful and enjoyable if you know why you are making it and what you want to do when you get there. Knowing this motivates you and gives you something to look forward to.

Take a few minutes to think about what it is that you would like to get out of this book. Is it one or more of the things below, or is it something else? Make a note of any of the reasons that apply to you, and any others, in a special notebook.

- ◆ You want to be happier.
- ◆ You want to be more successful.
- ◆ You want to find out how you can balance all the different areas of your life.
- ◆ You want help in your relationships at work or at home.
- ◆ You want to be more motivated.
- ◆ You want to become more confident and assertive.

Who are you?

You might be thinking 'What a strange question to ask – does it mean what is my name? Or where do I come from? Or what do I do?'

It is all of these things and more.

This is one of the first questions that delegates who attend our personal development course are asked. Often they are embarrassed to say anything at all about themselves let alone anything good! Many lower their eyes or look at the floor because they find it difficult to look at their fellow group members. They rush through their introductions so quickly and say so little that the rest of the group are left wondering if they are really that uninteresting!

Invariably they are not. Nobody is uninteresting – *nobody* – and this includes you. Many people appear uninteresting because they lack confidence or are embarrassed to talk about themselves and their achievements. This is particularly true of many British people who grow up in a country where it is not traditional to talk about themselves and their achievements. Americans are generally much more comfortable talking about themselves in this way but sometimes (especially for us shy, retiring Brits.) they go too far the other way and appear boastful or over-confident. Sometimes you can't win!

What makes you *interesting?*

To help you answer the question, think about what it is like when you meet someone for the first time, particularly when it is someone on whom you would like to create a good impression.

> Remember that at this first meeting the way you introduce yourself will provide the basis on which people begin to form their opinion of you.

Do you *honestly* think that the first impression *you* give to people is the one you would want them to have? Does it do justice to the real you?

This question requires you to think very carefully about yourself and who you are so that whenever you find yourself meeting someone for the first time – whether socially or professionally, whether one-to-one or in a group – you can introduce yourself confidently and without embarrassment. And, if the occasion calls for it, you can talk easily and fluently about your background, your achievements, your family and so on.

The following exercise is designed to help you create your own personal introduction, one that you can be proud of and that incorporates interesting and important information about you.

Try it now   Imagine that you have to introduce yourself to someone you have never met before. Your introduction should include details of your background, family, work and interests. To help you, you are asked to represent your life in a drawing – a picture or series of pictures – which illustrates your life and which will present a clear picture of who you are.

Think about this carefully and then do your drawing before reading any further. Use any size paper you wish and any type of drawing instrument (crayons, pens, pencils – whatever you feel easiest with).

Whilst you are drawing think about what words you would use to accompany each part of the picture to bring it to life. These words should create a positive and interesting image of you to your new acquaintance. For example if one of your hobbies is reading you might have illustrated this on your drawing as a book. When thinking about the words to accompany the picture do not just say 'I enjoy reading'. That doesn't say much about you at all. It's uninformative, very monochrome and it's boring! Talk about *what* you enjoy reading and why; 'I enjoy reading – my favourite authors are Thomas Hardy, Charles Dickens, Patricia Cornwell and Len Deighton. My favourite book is *Great Expectations* because...' this paints a much clearer picture of who you are (but don't go over the top or it will become self-indulgent and boring. Practice getting the balance just right).

Enjoy yourself – this exercise should be fun.

How did it make you feel?

The drawing exercise provides an insight into how you feel about yourself and how much you value yourself. Did you feel good? Nostalgic? Happy? Sad? Embarrassed? Proud? Motivated? If you felt good, positive and confident while you were doing it, particularly about the words that you used, then it is likely you would portray a confident and positive image to a new acquaintance.

However, if you felt embarrassed or nervous at the thought of having to talk to anyone about yourself in such detail then it may be that you lack confidence or do not value yourself enough. If that's how you feel then be warned – it will probably show whenever you introduce yourself.

This exercise can be of enormous help in getting you to focus on the important stages of your life. By doing the drawing and by putting words to it you have created a pictorial and verbal representation of who you are which can be stored in your memory. You never know when you may need to call on it, but it will be there for you to retrieve whenever you need it. Sometimes you may only need to recall *part* of the picture and *some* of the words (for example you might recall the bits about your career background if you are going for a job interview). But it will be there to help you whenever you need it.

Did you find it easy to do?

If you answered 'yes' to this question, try to get in touch with why you found it easy. Is it because you enjoyed doing it? Or perhaps you are used to doing this sort of thing because you often find yourself in situations when you need to talk about yourself? Is it because you are confident and have high self-esteem? Or is it because you didn't put much effort into it?! (If this is the case, have you done justice to yourself?) Is it because you are good at drawing? (If so, did you find the words came easily too?).

If you answered 'no' to this question, again try to get in touch with why. Is it because you don't think you have anything interesting to draw or to say about yourself? Or perhaps you don't think other people will be interested in you?

Or is it because you lack confidence or have a low self-esteem? (If this is the case you may have felt a bit embarrassed. particularly at the thought of having to *talk* about yourself.) How much effort did you put into the exercise? If you found it difficult, did you give up part way through it?

By getting in touch with how well you did in this exercise you are beginning to acknowledge a few truths about yourself. This will help you as you progress through the book and by the time you get to the end of it you should have a strong belief in your own worth. By nurturing the belief that *you* are important you will feel confident to talk about yourself and believe that your life is as interesting and as valuable as anyone else's. And you will be able to do this in such a way that you feel pride, not embarrassment.

Where are you now?

Do not take this question too literally! It doesn't mean are you in the sitting room or the bedroom. It means what stage are you at in your life?

> Analysing where you are now will help you to establish how close you are to where you *want* to be.

Once you know this you can begin to do something about it.

The questions below should help you to focus on where you are in your life at the moment:

What are the important areas of your life?

Think about which areas of your life are important to you, for example your family, holidays or work. List these in *descending* order of importance (i.e. list the most important thing first).

As you do this, think about whether you value each part of the area equally or whether there is a special part (or parts) within it that means more to you. For example, if you have written down 'family', is there a particular part of your family life that you value most – like, time spent alone with your partner at home – or do you value every part of your family life equally?

Make your own list now in your notebook. Put into words

any things that you particularly value within each area of your life.

Who are the most important people in your life, and why?

Write down the names of the people who are most important in your life and try to get in touch with what it is that makes each of these people important to you. Try to give as many reasons as you can. For example, 'My husband, because I love him, I enjoy being with him, we share many interests and he is my best friend.'

As you make your list ask yourself whether these people know how important they are to you, and why. Would you find it easy to tell each of them, or not? Or do you never tell them because you assume that they know?

In chapter six you will learn how expressing feelings is an important part of building a new future.

How much quality time are you spending in the areas of your life that you value the most?

Quality time is time that you spend doing something well or to a high standard – giving it your best effort and attention.

Think about the time that you spend in each of the areas that you listed above, and with the people who are important to you. Do you believe that you spend enough quality time in each of these areas – giving them your best effort and attention? Do you enjoy the time that you spend in these areas, or do you sometimes find that you have too much on your mind to enjoy it properly? For example, when you are with your family do you manage to relax and enjoy their company or are you constantly stressed and irritable because you are thinking or worrying about other things?

In answering this question you do not need to quantify the time in exact days or hours unless you want to – your answer should be more along the lines of 'I spend most of the weekend with my family, but very little of this is quality time because I am either watching something on the television or thinking about work.'

Write down your own answer now.

How content are you with your life at this moment?

Answer this question using the scale of contentment detailed below to rate how content you are with your life at the moment, both (a) at home and (b) at work (if you work). At the same time think about what it is that produces this level of contentment, and also what produces any element of discontent, and try to put it in words. This will help you to focus on the things in your life that you need to do something about if you are to choose a better life.

For example, 'I am happy 50% of the time at work because I basically enjoy what I do, especially meeting and helping people. The other 50% of the time I am unhappy because my manager frequently criticises me about things that have been done incorrectly, but rarely offers me any help or guidance on how to improve.' From this statement you can see that something needs to be done about the large area that is causing the discontent – the manager's constant criticism and lack of help.

As you progress through this book you will learn different techniques that will help you to enhance the areas of contentment by dealing with the areas of discontentment.

The purpose of this exercise is to get you to *begin* to focus on where you currently see yourself. It will help to establish the gap between where you are now and where you want to be. Write down your answers now.

Scale of contentment
1 = content with 0% – 25% of your life
2 = content with 26% – 50% of your life
3 = content with 51% – 75% of your life
4 = content with 76% – 100% of your life

What do you want out of life?

There are some important points to understand before you try to answer this question.

Be clear and specific about what you want

If you are unclear about what you want, or if you express it in a vague or non-specific way, you are unlikely to achieve it. This can lead to feelings of dissatisfaction, apathy, non-achievement and stress. For example:

I want to be happy

Although many people set this as one of their goals, it is far too vague to serve as a definition of what you want in life. You need to be clear about what happiness means to you and be very specific about it. For example, one of the things that would contribute to your happiness might be 'I want to have £10,000 in savings.' You will find that happiness comes *as a result* of achieving this and your other goals. It is *not* the goal itself. Happiness means different things to different people, hence it is important to define what it means to you.

There is more about setting goals later in the book.

I want to be successful

Again this is too vague: how do you define *successful*? Different people have different interpretations of the word. Someone who is very ambitious may define success as being Managing Director of a company. A housewife may define it as doing all of the housework *and* having quality time to spend with her family and her interests. Neither definition is right or wrong. What is important is to be clear about what success means to *you* in the role that you have.

I don't want to be doing this job in twelve months time

Although knowing what you *don't* want is the first step in acknowledging that something in your life is out of balance and needs to change, this, in itself, will not help you to get what you *do* want.

It does not express what you *want* to be doing, only what you *don't* want to be doing. As a result you may find that your mind will be focusing on negative thoughts and consequently your energy will be channelled into feelings of negativity, which can lead to stress, illness and so on.

Once you have acknowledged that you *don't* want something as part of your life, you need to take the next step which is to decide what you *do* want. For example 'I want to set up my own business making and delivering sandwiches to local businesses'. Only when you have done this can you begin to focus your energy – positive energy – into achieving it.

Be realistic about what you want

It is no good making a list of things you want to achieve if you know you stand no chance of achieving them. Or, if you are not prepared to put in the effort that it would take to achieve them. You must be prepared to take the responsibility for making things happen. If you are not prepared to take responsibility, re-think what it is that you really want.

For example, if you left school at 18 with qualifications in art and geography it is no good saying 'I want to be a veterinary surgeon' *unless* you are prepared to study and obtain all of the necessary qualifications. This is where you need to be honest with yourself – do you really want to be a vet or do you just want to work with animals? If you just want to work with animals, is there another, more realistic way of doing this or *are* you really prepared to study and qualify to be a vet? Would the challenge of studying motivate you, or do you dislike studying?

If you decide to go ahead with the studying, it is *your* responsibility to organise and put aside sufficient study time to achieve the qualifications. It is *your* responsibility to pay the costs – or to make arrangements to pay them.

So, in being realistic about what you want out of life, remember whether or not you are prepared to take on the responsibility that goes with it – are you prepared to pay the price?

Make sure that what you want is within your power

If you spend your life striving for something that is not within your power, you may end up very bitter, frustrated and disappointed. You may also end up transferring all of your energy into trying to achieve this impossible goal, at the expense of all else.

Let's take a closer look at what this means in the context of this book, because you could argue that theoretically nothing is totally within your power! The case study provides a common example of someone aiming for something that is not in their power.

Case Study _____

Jane was an intelligent young woman who had ambitions to be a writer and travel the world. She had carefully planned how she was going to achieve both of these ambitions and was prepared to put in the time and effort required. She was going to start in Canada, where she already had a job lined up and a place to stay.

But before she even got started on this she met John and fell head over heels in love with him. She started going out with him, although she knew that he was seeing other women too. She put up with it because it was a challenge and she believed that eventually he would finish with the others. She dropped her ambitions to write and travel because they would have taken her away from John. Her main ambition in life became John. She wanted more than anything to marry him and spend the rest of her life with him.

For four and a half years she put up with his two-timing and unreliability because she had built her whole future around him. During that time she was, in the main, very unhappy and insecure because she could not get John to marry her – or even get engaged. John tried to end their relationship several times, but each time she begged him to stay, always believing that things would be all right in the end.

But things never were 'all right' and, eventually, Jane realised that if she wanted any sort of future happiness it would not be with John. After nearly five years, and much heart break, she ended the relationship. Finding the strength to do this was one of the hardest things that she had ever done but it resulted in a very swift improvement in her life. She was happier at work, she made new friends (and regained many of her old ones who she had abandoned when she first met John!). Within twelve months she met and married the man who is still her husband sixteen years later – and she eventually achieved both of her original ambitions to travel and to write.

But for Jane the biggest lesson was that she had wasted almost five years of her life striving to achieve something that was out of her power – marriage to John. _____

This is what is meant by 'make sure that what you want is within *your* power'. If what you want out of life is largely in someone else's power you will not be in control of the situation and you will probably end up with only bitterness, frustration, jealousy and so on.

An even simpler illustration of setting a goal that is beyond your power is 'I want to win the lottery!' If you spend your whole life striving to achieve that, there is a very high chance you will end up disappointed. Why not channel your energies into something that is within your power, that you know you *can* achieve if you put the effort in? Ask yourself 'Why do I want to win the lottery? What would I do if I won it?' and channel your energy into achieving it *if* it's what you really want. If along the way you happen to win the lottery, then it will be a bonus!

Bearing in mind all of the above points, write in your notebook what *you* want out of life.

Summary

This first chapter has helped you to clarify where you are at the moment and where you want to be. You have done this by answering the following questions:

1. What do you hope to get out of this book?

2. Who are you?

3. Where are you now?

4. What do you want out of life?

In identifying what you want out of life you learned that it is important to:

◆ Be clear and specific about what you want.
◆ Be realistic about what you want.
◆ Make sure that what you want is within your power.

By now you should have built up a picture of how big the gap is between what you have got and what you want. This will also give you an idea of how much work you need to do.

In the next chapter you will be looking at some basic principles to help you build a better life.

CHAPTER 2

All things
whatsoever ye
would that men
should do to
you, do ye even
so to them.
(THE BIBLE,
MATTHEW 7:12)

Basic Principles for Building a Better Life

In seeking to build a better future, you need to be aware of certain aspects of human behaviour that can either help you or hold you back. By understanding some very basic, but important, principles and learning how they can help or hinder you, you will be in a very strong position to identify the style of behaviour that will be most beneficial to you.

You will also begin to better understand other people's behaviour which will help you in turn to know how best to respond to it.

Understanding human behaviour

Why is trying to understand human behaviour so important in helping you to build a better life? The simple answer is that human beings, in the course of their everyday lives, interact with other human beings. They go to work, fall in love, bring up children, and so on.

However, human behaviour is a complex psychological subject and whole books have been written on just *single* aspects of it. We are not going to study human behaviour in that much depth.

The aim of this chapter is to provide you with an insight into how certain aspects of behaviour – yours and other peoples – can affect your everyday life, for better or for worse! By understanding this you can choose how to use the knowledge you have gained and how to adapt aspects of your behaviour that are holding you back from getting what you want out of life.

As you read through this chapter please keep in mind the work that you did in chapter one. Think in particular about the gap that exists between where you are now in your life and where you would like to be.

Bear in mind too the wisdom in the words that exhort you to 'do unto others as you would have them do unto you'. Whatever your beliefs, your religion, your ethics, the power of these words cannot be denied.

> The message is perfectly clear – treat other people as you would want them to treat you.

The following six basic principles will be of enormous benefit in helping you to build a better life:

1. Be open and honest

'This above all: to thine own self be true
And it must follow, as the night the day,
Thou canst not then be false to any man'

(Shakespeare: Hamlet)

Another way of looking at this is to say 'Always tell the truth, there's less to remember!'

A survey, published in early 1997 by psychologists at the University of Southern California, discovered that the average person tells a lie every eight minutes – that's 180 lies a day! These range from little white lies like telling a beggar *'Sorry, I haven't got any change'*, to great big lies like *'Of course I'm not seeing anyone else'*.

Nobody wants to be continually lied to or kept in the dark so why is it, do you think, that some of the commonest complaints voiced about other people's behaviour relate to lies or lack of openness. *'He lied to me'*, *'She said she wouldn't do that again, and now she has'*, *'I wish my manager would tell me more about how the business is doing'*, *'If only I'd known what this job really entailed, I wouldn't have taken it'*.

It not only *hurts* when you find out you have been lied to, or kept in the dark, but it can also breed mistrust and disenchantment. Eventually it may also lead to you adopting the same style of behaviour because you have become conditioned to it as a way of life. Ask yourself the following questions:

◆ How many people do you know who are open and honest?
◆ Are *you* open and honest?
◆ How do *you* feel when you find out that someone has lied or deceived you or been less than truthful with you?
◆ How do you feel when *you* have lied or deceived *yourself*?

If you have trouble being honest with yourself, let alone with other people, then the first thing you need to sort out is *why*? What is it that you are deceiving yourself about? Is it a relationship that is not working out? Is it a job that you don't enjoy, or can't do? Go back and check the areas of your life you said you were dissatisfied with in chapter one and see if the answer lies there.

> Once you have got in touch with any areas of *your* life about which you are deceiving yourself, then you can begin to look at how open and honest you are with other people – and how open and honest they are with you.

Why do people lie?

Why do people lie? There could be a number of reasons, but often it relates back to the fact that telling a lie is an easier option than telling the truth. It might be something simple, like telling a friend that her new haircut looks good when you really think it looks awful. Or it might be something more complex, like telling someone who works for you that he stands a good chance of getting a promotion to a position that is soon to become vacant. In reality you tell him this because you don't want to demotivate or upset him by saying he is not suited to this higher position.

The consequences of lying

Let's just examine the consequences of these 'untruths'. The friend whose haircut you said looked good believes you and is then ridiculed by other people. By telling her the truth you would have given her the opportunity to do something about it – it becomes *her* responsibility and she has a *choice* of whether to change it or not. Lying to her, even if you justify it by saying you lied so as not to hurt her feelings, deprives her of that choice.

Instead of lying, why not try to find a tactful way of telling her what you really think – after all, she was the one who asked for your opinion in the first place so you should not feel guilty about giving it. You could say to your friend 'I don't think your new hair-style suits you as much as your old one. The blonde highlights are a bit overpowering'. By explaining it this way she not only knows *what* you think of her new haircut, but she also knows *why*. It is the 'why' that gives her the opportunity to weigh up what you have said and decide whether or not she wants to do anything about it.

In the second example, the possible consequence of the lie that was told is that the person who works for you is enthusiastic, happy and motivated until he finds out that he hasn't got the job. At first he is disappointed, then he finds out that you lied to him. He becomes resentful and bitter, his work standards might drop, he could tell other employees you are not to be trusted and create a general atmosphere of mistrust and demotivation. By telling the truth you could have avoided this situation and found other ways of motivating him that were more suited to his abilities. By lying, you have deprived him, and the Company, of this opportunity.

White lies

Let's look for a moment at the subject of 'white lies', which can be quite emotive and contentious. The fact is that white lies, even though often told with a good intention, are still lies and it is easy to fall into the habit of telling them and justifying your reasons for telling them. Do you find yourself falling into this habit?

If you answered yes, do you do it often, or just occasionally?

By making a bit more effort it is possible to find a way of telling the truth in a manner that should not cause hurt or offence. Telling white lies is a habit that can be broken if you want to break it.

However, let's acknowledge that there may be times when you feel a situation warrants a white lie. Where you believe that it is harmless or trivial, like telling a child that Father

Christmas exists. In situations like this ask yourself whether you would be doing more harm than good, or denying the child many years innocent enjoyment, by 'telling it as it is'.

If often takes strength and courage to tell the truth rather than a white lie. To help you understand this issue let's look at some of the more common ways that people try to justify telling a white lie:

(a) So as not to hurt another person's feelings

For example, telling white lies about someone's physical appearance, or the way they are dressed, or the standard of their work, or making excuses to friends or business acquaintances when cancelling arrangements.

(b) To protect *someone else* because you believe the truth would hurt too much

For example, telling white lies to protect a friend who is having an affair or whose partner is having an affair. Or to protect someone from knowing all the details when someone close to them suffers a serious illness.

(c) To protect yourself

For example, when you forget to buy bread and then tell a white lie by saying the shop had sold out. Or saying that you have read a memo in the office when all you have done is glance at it and pass it on because you thought it looked boring.

(d) To gain attention by 'colouring' or exaggerating your actions or achievements

For example, by saying 'I got *lots* of bargains (truth = three out of thirty items) when I went to the supermarket today. But it took me *ages* (truth = one minute) to get them back to the car. It was parked *miles* away (truth = 100 yards across the car park)'. The boy who cried wolf would fall into this category – and look what happened to him!

(e) For fun or for a joke

For example, telling a friend that she's got a big black mark on the back of her new white jacket. Or telling your partner you're going to the pub for a drink to celebrate his birthday when in fact you've organised a surprise party for him.

Consider this next point *very carefully*. Being totally open and honest all of the time could take some of the fun out of life – after all, who wants to deny a child (or an adult!) his fantasies? But in all of the above situations, how do you distinguish between a 'white lie' and a 'lie'? Where do you draw the line? How long is it before you find yourself justifying any lies using one of the above reasons? 'I only did it to protect myself'. 'I didn't want to hurt her feelings'. 'She'd have been devastated if she'd known the truth'. 'It was just a bit of fun'. 'I was only exaggerating a bit'.

Next time you find yourself in a situation where you are tempted to tell a white lie, stop and consider the option. Would it *really* be that difficult or harmful to tell the truth or be open about the issue? By making a bit more effort could you tell the truth and *still* be tactful or not cause offence? What would be the consequence of telling the truth. What's the worst thing that could happen?

> Have you got the *courage* to tell the truth and take the responsibility for facing up to the consequences?

Let's look at some examples of how it is possible to avoid telling a white lie and tell the truth instead.

Example 1

You are late for work one morning because you have overslept: your alarm went off at the normal time but you turned it off and went back to sleep.

◆ Your first option is to tell a white lie: 'Sorry I'm late – my alarm didn't go off', or '...the traffic was bad', or '...there was an accident', or '...my train was late.' Your justification for the white lie is that if you blame something that was beyond your control you won't get into trouble for being late.

♦ Your second option is to tell the truth: 'Sorry I'm late – I fell asleep again after my alarm went off (stating the facts). I'll work through my lunch hour to make up the lost time (taking responsibility).'

The worst thing that could happen is that you could lose your job. However, unless you have made a habit of being late for work the consequences are unlikely to be serious – you may get a reprimand. On the plus side, you are likely to win respect for your honesty (even if you still get reprimanded!).

Example 2

A married female friend is having an affair with someone at work. Her husband (who is also a friend of yours) tells you that his wife has been behaving strangely lately and he thinks she is seeing someone else. He asks if she has said anything to you.

♦ Your first option is to tell a white lie: 'No, she hasn't said anything to me.' Your justification for the white lie is 'She didn't actually *say* she was having an affair so I'm not really telling a lie', or 'I don't want to get dragged into this – it's their problem', or 'I don't want to hurt him.'

♦ Your second option is to tell the truth: 'If that's what you think then you should ask *her* that question. Please don't involve me in your personal affairs.'

In the second option you are being open with someone rather than telling them the facts about the situation. Even though you haven't told him that you know his wife is having an affair you have been open about how you feel about the situation and put the ball back into his (and his wife's) court. Effectively you are saying 'It's your responsibility to tackle your wife about it – don't try to transfer that responsibility to me'.

The consequences of telling the truth in this situation really depends on the individuals involved and your relationship with them. The worst thing that could happen is that you could lose the friendship of both your friends (but how strong a friendship was it anyway if this is the case?). However, it is more likely that the husband will keep on pestering you to tell him something (in which case you keep repeating that you do not want to get involved), or, he will tackle his wife about it and they will have to resolve the situation themselves.

The difference between being honest and being open

The above examples raise an important point about the difference between being *honest* and being *open*. Being honest means telling the truth. Being open is also about telling the truth and being above-board, *but*, sometimes this simply means stating your position or your feelings and nothing else.

Case Study ⎯⎯⎯⎯⎯⎯⎯⎯⎯⎯⎯⎯⎯⎯⎯⎯⎯⎯⎯⎯⎯⎯⎯⎯

A Company Director, because of his senior position, knows that there are going to be a number of changes taking place in his organisation over the next twelve months that will affect the employees and they have heard rumours that something is going to happen. These changes *may* involve redundancies or pay cuts and *may* also involve taking on new, better qualified, staff in order to move the Company forward. He is unable to give exact details yet and the Company does not want rumours flying around, or news of the changes leaking out to its competitors, until it is ready.

Being open with the staff in this type of situation means telling them 'There will be some changes in the Company in the next twelve months which will help us to move forward and be more competitive. At the moment I am unable to give you any more details because we are still looking at the best way to do this and nothing has been finalised. As soon as they have I will tell you more (always try to say when this will happen). I can assure you that any information you hear at the moment is only speculation'. ⎯⎯⎯⎯⎯⎯⎯⎯⎯⎯⎯⎯⎯

Now, this highlights an important point. If the Company Director in the above case study has a reputation for being deceitful or telling white lies then the workforce will not believe him. This may lead to instant demotivation and bad feeling. However, if he is a person with a reputation for being open and telling the truth, no matter how difficult, the workforce are more likely to believe him and accept what he's saying. They may still worry about the potential changes, but they are unlikely to be too demotivated at this stage.

Think about this cumulative effect very carefully next time you have to decide whether to tell the truth or tell a white lie –

your reputation may depend on it! In building a new future, it is up to *you* to make this decision.

> By being open and honest you are helping prevent the negative side of you from taking a hold.

The burden of living a lie can weigh very heavy – you will feel much 'lighter' when you tell the truth.

Try it now   Next time you speak to someone and you feel the temptation to tell a lie (white or otherwise.), or to exaggerate, or to mislead that person, *tell the truth* instead and see how it feels. Telling lies can become a habit – break it!

---

2. Trust and be trustworthy

'I prefer to have too much confidence and thereby be deceived, than to be always mistrustful. For in the first case I suffer for a moment at being deceived, and in the second I suffer constantly'
(Paul Gauguin)

Relationships built on trust stand more chance of success than relationships where trust is lacking. There are many benefits to be gained from being able to trust people.

◆ You see the good in people, not the bad.
◆ You feel at ease in the company of people you trust.
◆ You don't have to be on your guard all the time.
◆ You don't have to put up barriers.
◆ You don't have to be suspicious of everyone you meet or of their motives.

But how soon should you trust someone after you meet them? At the one extreme is it wise to trust everyone until they let you down? Or, at the other extreme, is it wise to never trust *anyone* until they prove that they can be trusted?

Perhaps the fairest way to treat people is to keep an open mind about them. That means you let them earn your trust by showing you that they are trustworthy but, whilst this is happening, try not to actively mistrust them (unless you have a valid reason for doing so).

By mistrusting people you can miss out on so much of the positive side of life. Think about how *you* would feel if everyone who met you mistrusted you until you proved that you could be trusted.

Building trust

So, what can people do to help build trust? For most people the following points will set a basic standard.

◆ Be open and honest 'Say what you mean, and mean what you say'.

◆ Do what you say you are going to do (or, if there is a *genuine* reason why you can't do it, remember to let people know).

◆ Form your own opinions and do not be swayed by someone else's prejudices – ('You can't trust him ...') unless they give you a good reason. Other people's prejudices are often based on their own unsatisfactory relationships. Just because your friend doesn't trust someone it doesn't automatically mean that you can't trust them. Always remember there are two sides to every story.

◆ Display positive body language (look people in the eye, but be careful not to stare or intimidate them).

How to handle being let down

Sadly some people will let you down very quickly, and sometimes very badly. To have your trust broken can be very difficult to come to terms with for some of us. It can lead to an automatic mistrust of everyone we meet or certain groups of people. For example, if a woman has been badly let down and betrayed by a man she may then automatically mistrust *all* men. The greater the betrayal, the deeper the mistrust.

Another potential side effect of having your trust betrayed is that it can make you bitter. Ironically, for some people, this leads them to treat other people the same way that they have been treated. For example, if a man has been seeing someone else behind his girlfriend's back, she may subsequently copy this behaviour with her next boyfriend (i.e. see someone else behind his back). Subconsciously she is getting her own back on her original betrayal by projecting her revenge onto an innocent man.

So what can you do about it when someone *does* abuse your trust? If you tackle it immediately in an open and honest way, the situation can in many cases be dealt with and is far less likely to happen again.

Example

You confide in a colleague that you are applying for another job and ask him not to mention it to anyone else. He assures you that he won't and you believe him. He then tells someone else, asking *him* not to tell anyone. But the person he tells then tells someone else, and so on. Before you know it, it has got back to your boss and proves very embarrassing for you.

You are faced with a choice:

(a) You can say *nothing* to the friend whom you trusted. But, as a consequence, you may bear a grudge, let his friendship go, decide to get your own back – all *destructive* and *negative* actions. You may also find that you project this mistrust onto other people and hence end up mistrusting everyone.

(b) You can make him face up to his actions. Ask him why he told someone else when he had said that he wouldn't. Tell him the consequences of his actions and how he makes you feel (more about how to do this effectively later in the book). This is a far more *constructive* and *positive* way of dealing with it and is likely to make him think twice before doing it again, either to you or to anyone else.

People who make a habit of abusing other people's trust (in a big or small way) often do it because they think they can get away with it – because they have done in the past. Many will think twice about doing it again if they know they will have to face the consequences.

If you mistrust people, or are untrustworthy yourself, you provide an opportunity for the negative person inside you to develop.

Try it now   1. Think of someone who you do not trust. Get clear in your mind why you do not trust that person. What would they have to do to (re)gain your trust? Help them to do it.

2. Think about anything you do that might lead people to mistrust you. Do whatever you have to in order to prevent this mistrust from arising.

---

3. Give people descriptive feedback to help them develop

'Just because you are making a noise in my direction, don't think you are communicating.'

(David Gordon)

Just as flowers need nourishment to help them develop and bloom, so people need nourishment to help *them* develop and bloom too.

Food provides physical nourishment, but in order to develop towards their full potential people need other types of nourishment too. For example, spiritual and mental nourishment. This fundamental need can be seriously underestimated.

Descriptive feedback

One very valuable way of obtaining mental nourishment is through descriptive feedback from other people. This can help people to understand what they are doing well, and also where they could do something better, or have a greater impact by doing something differently.

Good descriptive feedback provides an opportunity for personal growth. It should always be constructive, leaving the recipient in no doubt over what is said, because it will give factual evidence to support any comments. It should describe a person's *behaviour* and the impact of that behaviour on *you* rather than attacking the actual individual. If appropriate it should also state how that behaviour needs to change in order to help the person develop or have a greater impact.

◆ *'You've interrupted me three times now* (fact). *When you keep interrupting me it disturbs my train of thought* (fact) *and makes me irritable with you* (negative impact). *I'll be happy to listen to what you've got to say, but please listen and let me finish what I'm trying to say first,* (change in behaviour that needs to take place to improve the situation and have a positive impact).'

This is constructive, clear and descriptive. It makes it clear to the recipient how he has made you feel, what impact his behaviour has had, and how he needs to change this behaviour if he wishes to improve the situation. By giving him all this information he is able to weigh up the situation and the benefits of changing his behaviour.

An important point to remember is that descriptive feedback can also be given to let other people know what they are doing *well*, not just what they need to change.

◆ *'I liked the way that you dealt with that sales assistant* (positive impact) *when you returned the suit and asked for a refund* (specifies the situation). *You were polite but at the same time you made it absolutely clear that you weren't prepared to accept a replacement,* (states facts to explain why the behaviour had a positive impact).'

Feedback like this makes people feel good about themselves and helps build their self-esteem. It also makes them feel important and valued. Sadly, many people only tell you when you are doing something wrong (and they don't always do that very constructively!) – rarely when you do something well.

Giving clear, descriptive feedback to other people is something that you can try doing yourself as soon as the opportunity arises. Whether someone behaves in a way that upsets you, or whether someone does something well, have a go at giving them some descriptive feedback. Remember always to state facts, the effect the behaviour has on you and, if appropriate, what they need to change if they are to have an even greater impact on you.

It may feel a bit strange at first but don't let this put you off. When you master the art of giving descriptive feedback the benefit to both you and others will far outweigh any difficulty that you might have experienced. This is because you are helping to create an environment where people are encouraged to develop through understanding the impact that their actions have on others.

By encouraging other people to give you feedback this can

help you to value yourself more and can give you more ammunition to fight off any negative thoughts.

Try it now   Practise giving some descriptive feedback to someone close to you – a friend, colleague or loved one. Begin by explaining to them what you are going to do and why. Ask them to give you some feedback afterwards on how they felt and whether you could improve.

---

4. Be aware of any discrepancy between your intention and impact

'We judge ourselves by our intention, but we judge others by their impact.'

How aware are you of the impact that you have on other people? Can you be certain that what you say or do is heard or taken the way that you intend it to be?

By being aware of the impact that you have on other people and by making changes if necessary, you stand a much greater chance of achieving the things that you want in life. This is equally important whether at home or at work or in social situations.

Let's look at some examples of what is meant by impact and intention.

(a) A man says to a female colleague *'That's a lovely dress you've got on today'*. His *intention* was to pay her a genuine compliment. However, the *impact* of his words on her could be:

   ◆ You're paying me a compliment.
   ◆ You're being sarcastic.
   ◆ You're implying that I don't normally look good.
   ◆ You're chatting me up.

(b) A man sees some beautiful yellow daffodils in the flower shop and buys them to take home to his wife. His *intention* was quite simply to make her happy. The *impact* of his action on her could be:

   ◆ What beautiful flowers/what a lovely gesture. (Happy)

◆ Why are you buying me flowers? (Suspicion/ulterior motive)

◆ What have you done? (Mistrust)

It often takes someone else to point out the impact that you are having as you can innocently go through life being unaware of it.

Case Study _____

Chris, a sales manager, used to be very flippant. He thought that this flippancy was funny and clever. This belief was – in his mind – supported by the fact that, over a period of eighteen months since he became a manager, nobody had ever told him that he wasn't funny or clever. In fact the real impact of his flippancy on other people was either that nobody took him seriously or they thought that he was sarcastic. Soon after meeting him on a course the trainers gave him some descriptive feedback that his flippancy was having a negative impact on them. Other delegates also gave him similar feedback. He related this back to his work situation and his life in general. After acknowledging this he decided to change his behaviour. He was then taken much more seriously and gained respect that he had not previously had. He has not lost his sense of humour, just learned to use it more appropriately. _____

Unless you are sensitive to your impact on other people you could quite unintentionally end up doing more harm than good.

Try it now

1. From now on be aware of the impact that other people have on you. Try to ascertain why. Is it something they say, something they do, or a combination of both?

2. Be conscious of the impact you have on other people and try to ascertain why. Is it something you say, something you do, or a combination of both?

---

5. Avoid being critical and judgmental

> 'There's a lot of good in the worst of us,
> There's a lot of bad in the best of us,
> But it ill becomes any of us
> To talk about the rest of us.'
>
> *Thomas Carlyle*

Have you ever found yourself making a sweeping, judgmental comment or criticism about someone or something? *'That's rubbish'*, *'She's hopeless at her job'*, *'They think they're so much better than anyone else.'* Worse still, have you ever been on the receiving end of such a comment?

You may have come across people who seem to take enormous pleasure in finding fault with other people's lives *'I can't understand why she painted the kitchen yellow – it looks awful'*, *'He's going to Blackpool for his holidays again – you'd think he'd take the family somewhere else for a change'*, *'They must have the family visiting for Easter again – the street outside looks like a car park. You'd think they could all come in one car or park somewhere else.'*

Do you ever feel like saying to these people *'Can't you find something good to say for a change?'* or *'Who are you to judge others? We are all human and we all have our frailties.'*

How would *you* feel if you were on the receiving end of such comments? Angry? Hurt? Defensive? Want to make a similar comment in return? Sad? Puzzled? Not bothered?

Why do you think some people feel they have the right to make such sweeping judgments and criticisms? What makes them do it? There are a number of possible reasons:

◆ Jealousy.
◆ Conditioning. They've learned it from other people over a long period of time.
◆ It gives them a feeling of superiority. Often people who do it for this reason are insecure. They criticise other people – often to a third party – as it is the only way they can achieve this feeling of superiority and they know they are unlikely to be challenged.
◆ To gain attention. Again this is linked to insecurity and not valuing oneself. Because some people don't believe that they can gain attention in their own right they try to gain it by saying something that will make them the centre of attention. For example, someone joining the back of a long supermarket check-out queue says *'You'd think they'd do something about the length of these queues'*. Nine times out of ten he will gain the attention and agreement of all the other disgruntled shoppers in the queue. This makes him feel good. Again the

likelihood of being challenged is low because the comment is made to a third party. If asked for his suggestions on how to improve the situation it is unlikely that he would have an answer – the whole point of making the comment was to gain attention!

◆ Insensitivity. They don't consider the other people's feelings.

> Next time you find yourself about to make a judgmental comment or criticism, stop and think of something positive that you could say instead.

Instead of criticising the length of the supermarket queue you could say *'They're busy today aren't they! I'll remember to do my shopping at a different time next week to avoid the rush.'* Or, if you think there aren't enough check-outs open, bring this to the attention of the management rather than just moaning about it – they will do something about it unless they want unhappy customers!

And next time you hear someone else making a judgmental comment *challenge them* about it – don't go along with them. For example, if someone says *'She's got awful taste in clothes'* try asking *'Why do you say that?'*

The sort of person who frequently makes judgmental comments may have great difficulty when it comes to giving other people descriptive feedback to help them develop. The feedback is likely to be along the same lines as their comments – judgmental and critical and far from constructive. In fact it can often be *de*structive *'You didn't do that very well. Let me show you how it should be done.'* The impact can be that they are imposing their views on the other person rather than trying to help them. By imposing their views and opinions on other people they can so easily create a hostile and defensive environment.

> Judgmental feedback can be seen as a direct attack on the individual rather than his behaviour.

Judgmental feedback does not describe the behaviour that needs to be changed, nor does it give the individual any evidence to support the criticism:

♦ *'That sales presentation was useless!'*

or

♦ *'You look awful!'*

This is critical, opinionated and unhelpful. It can leave the recipient confused, angry, intimidated and can lead to him becoming defensive or blaming other people e.g. *'That's because you didn't give me time to prepare it properly'* or *'You don't look so good, yourself!'*

If people want to learn from each other in order to develop and succeed in life there is no place for constant sweeping criticism or unhelpful judgmental feedback. Next time you find yourself tempted to be critical or judgmental, think very carefully about how useful or effective your comments will be. Will they help the other person, or are they more likely to cause anger or offence? Ask yourself how *you* would feel and respond if *you* were on the receiving end of what you were about to say.

By judging others are you really judging yourself?

Try it now   Next time you feel the temptation to criticise someone, or make a judgmental comment, stop before you say anything. Try to make your point constructively – if you cannot do this, don't say anything!

Criticising and being judgmental can become a habit – break it!

---

6. Deal with issues before they become hidden agendas

'Unto whom all hearts be open, all desires known, and from whom no secrets are hid'

(*Book of Common Prayer: Holy Communion*)

Have you ever been in a situation where you have reacted uncharacteristically because someone has done something previously that has upset you and you have not dealt with it at the time?

Take the earlier example where you told a colleague that you were looking for another job and it eventually got back to your boss. If you did not deal with this at the time it is likely that you will hold it against your colleague and at some time in the future you will make sure that you get your own back:

Your colleague, at a later date, asks you to vote for him at the local Parent Teacher Association (PTA) where he is standing as school governor. Because he betrayed your trust in the past and you still hold this against him, you vote for someone else. Inside you shout *'Gotcha!'* – this is the chance you've been waiting for to get your own back! Naturally you don't tell him that you didn't vote for him – you probably even offer him your condolences when he fails to get elected. This give you great pleasure and a feeling of superiority.

This is a hidden agenda – a situation where *'I know why I'm doing something, but you don't.'* It is unlikely to resolve anything and it certainly will not create an open and honest environment.

Sometimes a hidden agenda can be very deep or go back a long way – you may not always be aware of it. It may need someone else to help bring it into your consciousness and thus help you to deal with it:

Example

Imagine that you have not been to any family gatherings at Christmas for over ten years. Although this is now accepted as the norm – i.e. your family no longer expect you to be there – this year your brother asks you why you won't be there. Your immediate reaction is to say *'I never go'*.

He persists *'Why not?'*

You respond *'I don't really know!'*

He asks *'Why did you stop going in the first place?'*

This sets you thinking – you may not be able to come up with the answer straight away. Then you realise that you stopped going because your mother always used to criticise your lifestyle and, even though it was done *'tongue in cheek'* this made you angry. You wanted to punish her and your way of doing this was to stop going to family Christmases because you knew this would hurt her – it was your way of getting your own back. But in reality you were really punishing yourself, so you were the loser.

But because nobody knew why – and you wouldn't tell

them – there was nothing they could do about it until it was brought into the open.

In a situation like that who do you think suffers the most? You, or your family, or all of you?

> Hidden agendas can be very destructive and can have an effect far beyond the original intention.

Hidden agendas can bury themselves so deeply that dealing with them becomes a problem because you are not really sure what they are about or why they are there. If you are guilty of having hidden agendas – and, let's face it, who hasn't been at some time in their life – please think very carefully about their effect. By dealing constructively with a situation straight away you can prevent so much bad feeling and pettiness.

Try it now	Next time you find yourself in a situation where, in the past, you might have let a hidden agenda arise, deal with the situation straight away and thus prevent any more from forming.

Summary

In this chapter you have learned six basic principles that will help you on your journey to building a better life:

- ◆ Be open and honest.
- ◆ Trust and be trustworthy.
- ◆ Give people descriptive feedback to help them develop.
- ◆ Be aware of any discrepancy between your impact and your intention.
- ◆ Avoid being critical and judgmental about other people.
- ◆ Deal with issues before they become hidden agendas.

All of these are principles that you can start to incorporate into your life straight away. They can help you to feel good about yourself and can encourage others to act likewise.

*If you always do
what you always
did, you'll
always get what
you always got.*

CHAPTER 3

The Power of Influence

T he next step looks at how you will begin to focus on the
things you do that have a positive influence and those
things you do that have a negative influence. At the same time
you will learn to become more aware of the things that *other*
people do that have a positive influence on *you* and those
things that *other* people do that have a negative influence on
you.

Why is this so important? Because the more influential you
become the easier it will be to lead the life you want.

Imagine what it would be like to approach every day of
your life in a positive way, knowing that you have the
power to cope with whatever happens.

You *do* have that power – it is up to you to choose whether
you use it. The influence you have on other people plays a
major part in this. If you have a positive influence you stand a
much greater chance of achieving a positive outcome. Whereas
if you have a negative influence this can hamper you every step
of the way – it may feel as if the whole world is against you!

In choosing a better life, you must first understand and
harness the power of positive influence.

How influence works

Let's begin by looking at how influence works. At a very early
stage of life when you were a baby and you wanted to be fed,
what did you do? The chances are that you cried – and you got
fed. So even before you could talk you were learning how to
use behaviour to influence your parents to get what you
wanted.

When you were a young child and you wanted something –
a sweet, a special toy, a new bike – you probably began to

realise that crying wasn't always the way to influence your parents. In fact it often had the opposite effect to what you intended and earned you a smack or a telling-off instead. So you learned that the same behaviour can have both a *positive* and a *negative* influence – it all depends on the circumstances. To confuse matters even further, you might have found that when *granny* was looking after you *she* gave you want you wanted if you cried. Confusing, eh?

You could have given up trying at that stage, or you could have realised that perhaps there were other ways of getting your parents to give you what you wanted – for example, smiling, laughing, hugging, tidying away your toys... but with granny it was crying that worked!

As you grew up and mixed with other people – at school, at work, and socially – you were exposed to many more positive and negative influences: from teachers, friends, colleagues or relatives. You learned a lot more lessons about what worked for you and what didn't. You made choices about what influenced you and what didn't. Can you remember the sort of people who influenced you most? Was it the bright ones who were always good at everything they did, or was it the naughty ones? Sadly, for many people, their formative years expose them to far more anti-influential behaviours (negative influences) than influential behaviours (positive influences) and this sets the pattern for the rest of their life.

Influence can be a two-edged sword

To understand the power that influence can have you need to acknowledge that it can be a two-edged sword. This means that you can just as easily be influenced by people who display anti-influential behaviours as by those who display influential behaviours. In fact the anti-influential behaviour often has the greatest appeal! The following case study relates to Frank, one of the authors:

Case Study _____

'Years ago I was a newly-appointed sales manager who had come to a cross-roads in my life. I was finding the job tough, I was having problems in my relationship with my manager, my confidence was low and I doubted myself.

Because I was feeling so low I was ripe to be influenced.

I knew a man who, like me, was a newly-appointed sales manager. He appeared always to be happy, spent money like water, always seemed to be going on holidays, had a fast car, was very popular with the women, and most of my colleagues looked up to him. I thought he was having the sort of life that I wanted: every day was a party. He had a very strong influence on me and I looked up to him as a role model.

I was very surprised and flattered to find that he wanted to spend time with me. I spent many hours in his company trying to do business, whilst wining and dining at some of the best places in London. I spent money that I did not have and went on holidays that I could not afford.

Because I enjoyed going out drinking with him this often led to me putting myself in a position where I knew that if I wanted to get home in the car I would have to drive under the influence of alcohol. I had often seen him do this without any problem and although I knew I was over the limit I did not want to appear weak in front of my hero. Soon this became a habit, and I justified it to myself by saying that I felt perfectly safe to drive and I had never had an accident.

Inwardly I was beginning to hate myself because I realised that this was not the life I wanted. But outwardly I was unable to escape from the power he held over me because I was using him to help me escape from the real world and the realities in it. I had not faced up to my responsibilities – to get on with my job and sort out my relationship with my manager. It took a close friend to tell me that I was changing for the worse to make me realise I was on a slippery slope to financial ruin and alcohol abuse. I had to break away from my role model's influence which I had come to realise was negative.

I did this by moving to another Company. When I subsequently rationalised what he was really like I saw that he was an alcoholic who was jealous, insincere, arrogant, envious, aggressive and blamed others for his shortcomings. However because of my own state of mind at the time, I had been influenced by these anti-influential behaviours which I had mistakenly seen as being the answer to my own shortcomings.

With hindsight I wonder how I could ever have seen him as a friend and a role model. For me this was a big lesson in the power that anti-influential behaviours can have. The frightening thing was that it felt exciting at the time!' _____

The above case study is an excellent illustration of how the power of influence can work on people in a destructive way. We let ourselves believe that anti-influential behaviours are acceptable because they are exciting or they achieve the result that we think we want.

But beware! Rarely do they give any long term satisfaction. In fact they often breed further anti-influential behaviours in us. We *blame* our former role models and others for the pain and suffering that they have caused us because that takes the responsibility away from us!

Breaking the mould

Think about how many people you know who waste energy moaning, criticising and passing judgment on others. Remember what you read about this in chapter two. People see this behaviour displayed on the television and in the newspapers too so it becomes the norm. It's easier to follow the norm than it is to be the one who breaks the mould.

But if you *want* to break the mould in order to have a more positive influence and a better life, you can. Let's look at what it takes.

> Part of living a happier, more fulfilled life is understanding what you do that has a positive and a negative influence on others and what others do that has a positive and a negative influence on you.

Only by acknowledging this, building on your influential behaviours and getting rid of your anti-influential behaviours, can you begin to benefit from its effect.

The following two exercises will get you to focus on behaviours, characteristics and qualities that can have a *positive* influence, and the behaviours, characteristics and qualities that can have a *negative* influence. There are a number of words listed below which describe these. You can probably think of other words that *you* would like to add to the lists.

The purpose of these exercises is to help you identify things you do – or don't do – that prevent you from being influential and can thus hold you back from getting what you want out of life. As you read through the lists think very carefully about each word and ask yourself honestly whether you display this behaviour, characteristic or quality:

◆ always
◆ sometimes
◆ never.

Exercise

The list of words that appears below describes some *influential* behaviours, characteristics and qualities. In your notebook write *'influential behaviours'* at the top of a page, then divide the page into three columns, headed

1. 'Always'
2. 'Sometimes'
3. 'Never'.

Read through the list below very carefully, and decide whether you feel each of the words could be applied to *you* 'always', 'sometimes' or 'never'. Then write it down in the appropriate column.

Honest	Open	Assertive
Polite/courteous	Trustworthy	Kind
Caring	Loving	Rational
Good sense of humour	Unselfish	Punctual
Confident	Smart appearance	Positive attitude
Gives praise/ encouragement	Good listener	Good eye contact
	Motivated	Supportive
Involves others	Sensitive	Understanding
Focused	Sincere	Constructive
Enthusiastic	Forgiving	Calm
Good communicator	Open-minded	Smiling
Admits mistakes	Respectful	Decisive

When you have finished the exercise above, ask someone whose judgment you respect to read through the list. Do they agree with what you have written, or do they perhaps see you differently? For example, you might have written 'Good listener' in the 'Always' column, whereas someone else might feel this would be in the 'sometimes' column.

Ask them to tell you *why*, making sure that they do this descriptively and constructively – remember what was said in chapter two about descriptive feedback. The more people you can get to do this, the better the picture you can begin to build of the influence you have on other people.

You will return to this list in the next chapter.

Exercise	The list of words that appears below describes some *anti-influential* behaviours, characteristics and qualities. In your notebook write '*anti-influential behaviours*' at the top of a page, then divide the page into three columns as before headed:

1. Always
2. Sometimes
3. Never.

Read through the list below very carefully and decide whether you feel each of the words could be applied to *you* 'always', 'sometimes' or 'never'. Then write it down in the appropriate column.

Rude/discourteous	Flippant	Aggressive
Sarcastic	Late/poor time-	Inconsiderate
Selfish	keeper	Lacks confidence
Negative attitude	Weak	Blames others
Too talkative	Moans	Closed-minded
Poor eye contact	Over-apologetic	Unkind
Untidy appearance	Arrogant	Tells tales out of
Gossip	Lack of control	school
Tells lies	Spiteful	Uses bad language
Jealous	Indecisive	Critical
Has hidden agendas	Envious	Bears grudges
Waffles	Judgmental	Doesn't admit
Disrespectful	Doesn't listen	mistakes
Interrupts	Shouts	Short-tempered
Demotivated	Unfocused/lacks	Irrational
Insincere	direction	Plays victim*

*People who *play victim* do not accept responsibility for the results of their actions – they say things like '*It's not my fault*' or '*I'd have done it better if you'd shown me how to do it properly*'. When things go wrong these people go around blaming others and feeling sorry for themselves rather than accepting responsibility and trying to find a constructive solution.

Again, ask someone whose judgment you respect to read through and comment on your lists – as in the first exercise.

Given a choice, most people prefer to display the influential behaviours, characteristics and qualities listed in the first exercise – and to be in company of other like-minded people. Why then do so many people fall into the habit of displaying the behaviours, characteristics and qualities described in the *anti-influential* list – or not fully utilising those described in the *influential* list?

Why?

Look at the words in the anti-influential list that appear in the 'sometimes' and 'always' columns. These describe behaviours, characteristics and qualities you have said you actually display – whether it is always or only sometimes. If you agree that these words all describe negative behaviours, characteristics and qualities *why do you let them form a part of your life?* Is it for one of the following reasons?

- That's what you've always done.
- It seems like the easy option.
- You believe it's the best way to get things done.
- Other people do it that way.
- That's how you were taught to do it.
- You want to be manipulative.
- You lack confidence.
- You like the power that it gives you.
- You don't really understand why.

How many times have you cringed when you've seen other people displaying anti-influential behaviours, only to do exactly the same yourself?

Think of someone you know who displays a large number of anti-influential behaviours – it may even be you! Think about the sort of impression that person creates:

- Unfriendly/unapproachable.
- Bully.
- Bossy.
- Manipulative.
- Opinionated.
- Not the sort of person I'd want as a friend.
- Cold.
- Nasty.
- Depressing to be with.

♦ Insecure.
♦ Weak.

You can probably think of a lot of other words but one thing is for certain, collectively they describe the sort of person that most people would choose to avoid. The more anti-influential behaviours a person displays, the less positive influence he is likely to have.

Let's just enter a word of caution at this point. Someone who is manipulative can appear to be using influential behaviours whereas in reality he is only using them to serve his purpose – they are used to mask his real intention.

For example, think of the salesman who smiles, is polite and appears very caring and understanding about your needs – right up to the moment that he sells you something. Once the sale is made the situation can be very different, particularly if you find yourself wanting to return the product or cancel the contract. You may now discover that he displays none of these influential behaviours – he had just used them to manipulate you into buying something!

When people display anti-influential behaviours, the impact they have on others is likely to be negative. And if they continue to display these behaviours they will continue to have a negative impact. In other words, *'If you always do what you always did, you'll always get what you always got.'*

> Next time you meet someone, try to identify the influential and anti-influential behaviours they are displaying. By consciously studying these behaviours you will find it can help you to identify why someone is having a positive or a negative influence on you.

If you think someone is *boring*, try to identify what it is that is giving this impression. Is it one or more of the anti-influential behaviours on the list? You may be surprised by what you find. Often it is only one or two things that are creating this impression – but they are showing so strongly that they are having a negative influence on you. You may identify that the person is boring because he *talks too much* and *doesn't listen.* You are then in a position to decide whether you want to deal with this issue and thus try to help him have a more positive influence on you. Because you have identified the offending behaviour, you can pinpoint exactly what is causing the negative influence and be constructive in any feedback you give (more about this in chapter four).

Summary

In this chapter you studied a list of influential behaviours, characteristics and qualities and identified which of these apply – or don't apply – to you. You learned that when other people display influential behaviours then the influence they have on people is likely to be *positive*.

Next you studied a list of anti-influential behaviours, characteristics and qualities and identified which of these apply – or don't apply – to you. You learned that when other people display anti-influential behaviours then the influence they have on people is likely to be *negative*.

CHAPTER 4

I can complain because the rose bush has thorns, or I can rejoice because the thorn bush has roses.

Harnessing the Power of Influence

In this chapter you will learn how you can get out of the habit of using anti-influential behaviours and into the habit of using influential behaviours. The benefits are a better life for you and for the people around you.

Dealing with anti-influential behaviours

Assuming you want to get rid of your anti-influential behaviours, how are you going to do this?

First look back at the words that you wrote in the 'always' and 'sometimes' columns from the anti-influential list. You may find that it is making you feel negative just looking at them. And no wonder, because what you are acknowledging is that it has taken you a lifetime to build up a set of behaviours that you don't like – you have become conditioned to behave this way!

The good news is that there is a *very simple* technique that can help you to change all of the anti-influential behaviours that you display. By following it you can attack and destroy each of these behaviours immediately *if you want to*. Try using the following technique on each of the anti-influential behaviours that you have written in the 'always' and 'sometimes' columns and you will experience for yourself how simple it can be.

Step 1. Think of a time when you displayed this anti-influential behaviour. Remember what you did and how you were feeling at that time.

Step 2. Think of an alternative and *positive* behaviour that you *could* have used.

Step 3. Ask yourself what made you choose the anti-influential, negative behaviour over the positive behaviour?

Step 4. Think about what you can do in future to ensure that you always choose to use the positive behaviour over the negative behaviour.

Example

Let's look at an example of how to apply this technique. We'll use a behaviour that you have probably come across time and time again and that you might also have been guilty of yourself in the past – *moaning*.

Step 1

Think of a time when you displayed this anti-influential behaviour. Remember what you did and how you were feeling at that time. Maybe, for example, you arrived home from work and your partner asked you what sort of a day you had. Straight away you launched into a catalogue of moans about what an awful day it had been and how fed up you were – and how nothing seemed to go right. You felt really down and demotivated.

Step 2

Now think of an alternative and positive behaviour that you could have used.

◆ You could have said '*I've had a bad day, but it's over now. How was your day?*' and smile.
◆ You could have focused on something positive – however small – that happened during the day. For example '*I met Susan for lunch and we had a great chat.*'
◆ You could have explained that some of it was good and some of it not so good. You could perhaps have asked your partner if you could discuss the *not so good* bits in order to talk through them and see how you could have handled them differently.

This approach gives you the opportunity to air your feelings and as such can be quite therapeutic. However it is important to do it with a positive intention otherwise it reverts to moaning!

By thinking and talking about how you could have dealt with the situation differently you are creating the right environment to prevent it from happening again and thus avoiding the need to moan about it again.

Step 3

Now consider what made you choose the anti-influential, negative behaviour over the positive behaviour. This step of the technique requires you to be *very* honest with yourself and to *take responsibility* for your behaviour. In other words, don't blame other people or outside influences for making you behave the way you did. If you do that, you are using another anti-influential behaviour (blaming others) as an excuse. It was *your* choice to behave the way that you did – the sooner you can accept responsibility for making that choice the sooner you are creating an environment in which you can change it.

In this example the reason for choosing the negative behaviour over the positive behaviour could be:

◆ It's a bad habit that you have fallen into.
◆ It's easier to be negative than it is to be positive.
◆ It felt like the natural thing to do.

Do not make excuses like:

◆ Nothing ever goes right for you.
◆ Your boss always picks on you.
◆ Nobody understands you.
◆ The Company does not value you.
◆ Everyone else moans about work.

Can you see the difference between the first set of reasons and the second set? The first set is being honest with yourself and taking personal responsibility, which is far more likely to lead to change for the better. The second set is blaming others and playing victim which is unlikely to lead to change.

If you want to get yourself out of the habit of using the anti-influential behaviours it is important and vital that you look on everything in a positive way.

> The only thing stopping you from being positive is *you!*

Step 4

Think about what you can do in future to ensure that you always use the positive behaviour over the negative behaviour. You can:

◆ Adopt a positive attitude.

◆ Focus on the positive aspects of a situation, however small.

◆ Take steps to prevent the situation that caused your anti-influential behaviour from arising again. Deal with anything that goes wrong, or with any negative issues, as soon as they happen. Confront the situation, however uncomfortable, rather than avoiding it or moaning about it later.

For example, if the reason for your bad day at work was that your boss shouted at you because you were late submitting a report, deal with this situation straight away. Explain *why* the report was late giving *facts*, not *excuses*. Discuss any changes that need to happen to ensure that the situation does not arise again – it may be that you need an extra day to assimilate all of the figures effectively – and assure him that it will not happen again.

◆ Pause and think before speaking. By consciously stopping yourself from moaning you will find that it progressively becomes easier to drop the habit. If you can't think of anything positive to say, don't say anything!

◆ Think of the impact your behaviour has on the other person. How will your moaning make the other person feel? How would *you* feel if you were in their shoes?

> The sooner you start to use this technique to confront your anti-influential behaviours the sooner you will feel and see the benefits.

It's all up to you. One thing is for certain – other people will notice the difference and you'll be surprised how quickly some will begin to follow your example. At the same time you should find that you begin to feel better about yourself and your environment.

Try it now   Pick one of the anti-influential behaviours from your 'sometimes' or 'always' column. Use the above technique to help you discover which influential behaviour you could have used instead. Write your answer in your notebook.

Focusing on influential behaviours

Now that you have looked at a way of dealing with your anti-influential, negative behaviours it's time to look at a way that will help you to focus on, and implement more, of the influential, positive behaviours.

Turn to your list of influential behaviours in your notebook. Focus on the words in the 'never' and 'sometimes' columns.

If you agree that these words all describe positive, influential behaviours, ask yourself why you don't let them form a part of your regular behaviour pattern and thus begin to harness the power that influence can bring.

Do you admire or respect other people who display positive, influential behaviours? Does it make you feel good when you use these behaviours?

Think of someone you know who displays a large number of influential behaviours. Think about the sort of impression that person creates – some of the following words will probably come to mind:

◆ Friendly/approachable.
◆ Helpful.
◆ Kind.
◆ The sort of person I'd want as a friend.
◆ Inspirational.
◆ Good company.
◆ Strong.
◆ Good leader.
◆ Charismatic.

Would you like people to think of you in some or all of these ways? The ability to display all of the influential behaviours is within your power – remember what was said earlier: the choice is yours and nobody else's.

You can use a very similar technique to the one you have just looked at to help you implement more of the influential behaviours. All you need to do is replace the first two steps so that the technique looks like this:

Step 1

Think of a time when you *could* have used an influential behaviour but you didn't. Remember what you did and how you were feeling at that time.

Step 2

Think about which anti-influential behaviour you used and which influential behaviour you could have used instead.

Step 3

Ask yourself what made you choose the anti-influential, negative behaviour over the positive behaviour?

Step 4

Think about what you can do in future to ensure that you always choose to use the positive behaviour over the negative behaviour.

Example

Let's look at an example of how the technique works on influential behaviours using *courtesy* to demonstrate the technique.

Step 1

Think of a time when you could have used an influential behaviour but you didn't. Get in touch with what you did and how you were feeling at that time.

Imagine you are out shopping and you are just leaving the bookshop through a swing door. Even though you see a lady a little way behind you with her arms full of shopping bags you let the door swing closed rather than waiting and holding it open for her.

Step 2

Now think about which anti-influential behaviour you used and which influential behaviour you could have used instead.

The anti-influential behaviours that you used were *rudeness* and *discourtesy*. You may also feel that a few other anti-influential behaviours apply to this situation too: selfish, arrogant...

An influential behaviour that you could have used instead was *courtesy*.

Step 3

Ask yourself what made you choose the anti-influential, negative behaviour over the positive behaviour?

Remember that this step of the technique requires you to be very honest with yourself and to take responsibility for your behaviour. In other words, don't blame other people or outside influences for making you behave the way you did.

In this example the reason for choosing the negative behaviour over the positive behaviour could be:

◆ You were in a hurry.
◆ You didn't think.
◆ You couldn't be bothered.

Do *not* make excuses like:

◆ Someone did it to you on the way into the shop.
◆ She should walk faster.
◆ It's not your job to hold the door open.

Step 4

Think about what you can do in future to ensure that you always choose to use the positive behaviour over the negative behaviour.

In this type of situation, if you act fast enough, you can apologise to the lady and at least try to redeem yourself! In *future* you could:

◆ Be more patient.
◆ Think how you would feel if you were in the other person's shoes: it is likely that you would be annoyed or frustrated if someone let the door go in your face, whereas if they waited and held the door open for you it is likely that you would feel pleased and grateful.
◆ Treat others the way you would want them to treat you.

Try it now   Pick one of the influential behaviours from the 'sometimes' or 'never' columns. Use the above technique to help you discover how you could have used this behaviour instead of an anti-influential behaviour. Write your answer in your notebook.

Sadly conditioning often leads people down the path of the negative, anti-influential behaviours. For example, if you had been brought up in an environment where it was not the done thing to hold doors open for other people it is quite likely that you would be conditioned to behave that way yourself.

However, by now you should have an understanding of the power of positive influence and the fact that the choice of whether to use a positive or a negative behaviour is *yours*.

> It takes the same amount of energy to use the positive behaviours as it does to use the negative ones.

The power of being a good listener

'Let every man be swift to hear, slow to speak, slow to wrath.'
(James 1:19)

There is something else that can help you even more to harness the power of influence. Something that is theoretically very easy to do. Something that everyone could benefit from at one time or another.

Yet in practice many people fail to do it. The doctor with his pen poised to write out a prescription at the first opportunity, often fails to do it. The salesperson who can't wait to tell you how good his product would be for you, fails to do it. The friends who have all the answers to your problems before you've even told them what your problems are, fail to do it.

It is known as *active listening*. 'Active' because it means that you need to make a conscious effort to listen and understand what is being said – giving encouragement when appropriate. By listening actively – as opposed to being passive and letting events take their course – you can make the speaker feel much more valued and important. Listening actively gives the impression that you really care about what the other person has to say.

Sadly many people tend to talk much more than they listen. After all, what could be more interesting than the sound of their own voice! When they do listen it is often only to hear what they want to hear or to listen for cues to take over the conversation.

> Listening, if it is to be an effective skill, should be an active process which, for most people, requires practice.

When was the last time that someone *really* listened to you? Or the last time that you *really* listened to someone else. How often do people *really* listen to other people?

It's a sad but true fact that listening is often done in a half-hearted fashion, with the listeners paying as much attention to thinking about or rehearsing their response as they do to what the speaker is saying. To illustrate this point let's look at two examples:

Example 1

If you look at a group of people in a pub or a restaurant you will often see that the only person each group member is interested in is himself and what *he* has to say.

It is likely that there will be numerous occasions when you will see a group of people all talking at the same time, or talking across each other, or interrupting each other. If you listen to them you may often notice that they are just waiting for someone else to give them a cue to take over the conversation. They then turn it to their advantage – '*Oh, you've just got back from a holiday in Orlando. I went there last year. I'm going to Cyprus this year...*' and then another person takes over. '*I was in Cyprus three years ago...*' and so it goes on. Before they know it they've been around the world but no-one was really interested in what anyone else was saying, only in their own contribution!

The following conversation illustrates the point beautifully – in fact it illustrates several points:

Man A:	'*Have you had a busy week?*'
Man B:	'*Yes, it's been really busy. My legs are really aching from all the kneeling down...*'
Woman (interrupts):	'*I get like that too sometimes. I've been the same ever since Amanda was born. It's a real nuisance when I'm trying to do the housework...*'

Man B (ignoring woman):	'It's been really wet this week too...'
Woman (interrupts):	'I know. My arthritis has been awful. I can tell as soon as the weather starts to change...'
Man B (to Man A):	'Have you been busy?"
Man A:	'Quite busy. I was up early this morning.'
Woman (jumps in before Man B has a chance to speak):	'I got up with him and made a cup of tea. I had a piece of toast when he'd left the house, then I caught up with some paperwork...'

And so it went on!

There are quite a few points to think about here:

◆ The woman appears to be desperate for attention – why? Is it perhaps because she feels nobody takes an interest in her? Or maybe because she wants to feel she can make a valuable contribution?

◆ Who is most at fault in this example – the woman for interrupting, or the men for totally ignoring her attempts to join in? How could they have handled this differently? Should they have asked her not to interrupt them – making sure they then let her have her say at the end? What would you have done?

◆ Did anyone in this conversation realise what they were doing, or are they all conditioned to behave in that way and therefore they don't actually realise – or care – what they're doing? How would they react if someone replayed the conversation to them and showed them what had taken place?

◆ Did anyone in this group consider the feelings of anyone else? How did the woman feel when she was ignored? How did the men feel when they were interrupted? Or are they all so engrossed in their own self importance that they don't really care about anyone else's feelings? Relate this to what you learned about influential and anti-influential behaviours in chapter three and earlier in this chapter. Also think about how impact and intention come into play in such a situation.

It is very interesting when you see, or experience, such interactions to try to get to the bottom of why they happen. By understanding each person's motivations, or possible motivations, you can hopefully prevent yourself from falling into the same trap. Next time you are in a pub or a restaurant, watch and see the interactions between people in a group. You'll be amazed how many talk or interrupt but don't listen!

Example 2

Have you ever listened to a sales person trying to sell something? It might have been on the telephone, or in the bank, or in a shop, it might even have been in your own home.

Sales people have a job to do – to sell a product. They normally know a lot about the product and can go on all day about how wonderful it is. They might think they're being interesting, but do *you*? Are you really interested in the fact that the video recorder a salesman is trying to sell you has a two-week programmable timer when you've just told him that you only want to use it for watching pre-recorded videos?

How many sales people are actually interested in *you* and what *you* want? How many sales people can you honestly say have ever really *listened* to you before trying to extol the virtues of their product? If your experiences with sales people are anything like ours, the answer is very, very few.

The vast majority of them give the impression that they are only interested in themselves and what they have to sell. Very few genuinely appear interested in *you* or what you want. It appears that only a few sales people – the best ones – take an interest in their customers. That's what makes them the best!

Case Study _____

The telephone rang and I answered it. Despite the fact that I am female – and my voice on the telephone sounds female! – I was greeted by a young man with the following words: 'Hello, is that *Mr* Jones?'

Straight away he's off to a bad start with me – my impression of him is that he's got my husband's name out of a telephone directory, written it down at the top of his script, and hasn't even bothered to listen when I've answered the telephone.'No, Mrs Jones actually!'

'Oh...sorry. I'm Steve from S... Windows. We're doing a promotion in your area at the moment and we're offering to double-glaze your property at a very substantial discount if you let us photograph it and use it in our promotional literature...'

'Let me stop you there. We've already got double-glazing, thank you.'

Unperturbed, he ploughs on reading from his script before he realises what I've just said.

'It's at a fraction of the normal price...Oh, are you *sure* you've got double-glazing?'

Now he's really irritated me, 'I'm very sure – we built our own house and helped put the windows in ourselves.'

'Oh. So you're not interested?'

'No thank you. Goodbye.' I put the phone down.

Let me ask you something – do you really think he was in the least bit interested in what *I* wanted? Or was he more interested in the commission he stood to earn if he signed me up, or in making sure he said all the words in his script?' _____

Perhaps you have had a similar experience to the woman in the case study. How did it make you feel?

Fortunately not all sales people are like Steve, and when you come across a sales person who *does* take a genuine interest in you and what you want, it can be a refreshingly pleasant experience. It feels good and it makes you much more interested in listening and buying the product.

Good listening skills are difficult to describe, but can be very influential when you are on the receiving end of them. Think about the excellent work that the Samaritans do by actively listening to people who have problems. Without this listening ear many of the people who call the Samaritans would not have anyone to talk to. For some of them it makes the difference between life and death.

By being able to talk to a person who is genuinely interested in listening to you it can help you to express your feelings. It can help you to talk through new ideas or clarify what you want to do about a particular issue, or it can help you to deal with any negative feelings and experiences that are holding you back. Active listening can be a tremendously influential behaviour but it is only useful in influencing if the listener is *genuinely* attentive and respects the other individual.

> When you have sincere willingness to listen to others, to regard them and their feelings as important, then they are also likely to treat you with the same respect.

How to be a good listener

Do you consider yourself to be a good listener who is genuinely interested in what other people have to say? If not, or if you need help to improve your listening skills, the following points should help you. If you want to be a successful listener there are certain things that you are encouraged to do and certain things that you should avoid. First we will look at the things you *should* do that will help you to be an effective active listener.

Maintaining good eye contact

Always try to maintain good eye contact with the person who is speaking. This indicates that you are paying attention to what they are saying and it also gives you the opportunity to watch their actions and reactions – to see if their words and body language are saying the same thing.

> You do not need to be an expert in body language to see if someone is comfortable or uncomfortable with what they are saying!

If you do not maintain good eye contact with the speaker – for example you frequently look at the floor, or out of the window, or at your watch – you are unlikely to encourage the speaker to open up. Additionally it increases your chances of being distracted by something that catches your eye. Once you've been distracted it can be difficult, if not impossible, to listen *actively* to what is being said because your mind is elsewhere. There is also the danger that whilst you are distracted you miss a point that the speaker is making. As a simple example, the speaker says 'We went to Greece for our holidays this year'. You have not been listening properly because you were distracted by a cat trying to catch a bird in the tree outside the window. Later you say 'Did you go anywhere nice for your holidays this year?' Whoops! How do you think this is going to make the other person feel? And it may not always be something as simple as a holiday that you fail to hear about.

Think how you would feel if someone did that to you when

you were trying to say something. It is so important to let the person who is speaking know that you are interested in what they are saying, and maintaining good eye contact is one way to do this.

A word of caution! Good eye contact does *not* mean *staring*. This is likely to make the speaker feel uneasy and clam up. Try to be conscious of the impact you are having on the speaker and adjust your eye contact accordingly.

Clarifying a point

When you really listen to someone you may find that they sometimes get their facts a bit mixed up. This may be completely unintentional, or it may be that they are telling a lie. By picking them up on it you will give them the opportunity to hear back what they have said and to put it right.

For example, the person speaking might begin by telling you that he worked abroad for three *years*, then later he may state this as three *months*. By pointing out that 'You said earlier that you worked abroad for three *years*, now you've just said three *months* – which was it?' you are giving him the chance to clarify the point.

Alternatively you may need to clarify a point in your own mind if you do not fully understand what the speaker is saying. This should ensure that you can give your full attention to what is subsequently said rather than worrying about an earlier point that was puzzling you:

'Before you go any further can I just clarify something? You said that you went to Canada to stay with your sister, but I thought that you were an only child.' 'Oh sorry – I meant my half-sister: my dad's been married twice. His first wife is dead now, but they had two daughters so I've got two half-sisters.'

Asking questions with care

However, not everyone finds it easy to open up or to express their feelings and if there comes a point when the speaker appears to '*dry up*' you may need to give encouragement to continue or to expand on a point.

Simple questions like:

◆ *'Tell me more...'*
◆ *'How did you feel when that happened?'*
◆ *'Why do you think that?'*

are often enough to encourage the speaker to say more. Never be afraid to ask someone to give you more information – it has several benefits:

◆ It can help you to understand them better.
◆ It can help you to understand their point of view – you don't have to agree with it, but it may help you to understand it better.
◆ It can help them to voice feelings that they may have been holding back for a long time.
◆ It can often help them to find a solution to whatever is troubling them.

Ask questions to help you understand the speaker's point of view, not necessarily to help you *win the argument*. Take care that the *urge to win* does not prevent you from listening.

> Remember that the main purpose of active listening is to give *someone else* the chance to talk through something that is on their mind.

Acknowledging the speaker's feelings

The more you listen to people, the more you are likely to find that they are prepared to open up to you. Often this involves expressing deep-rooted feelings that they may have found difficult to express previously. They may be feelings of anger, hatred, sadness, excitement... Whatever they are, always try to acknowledge them.

Often you will reflect their feelings in the way you look – you may look sad or happy or excited in the same way that they do. This can create a tremendous feeling of empathy.

Never say things like 'I understand what you're going through'. 'I know how you feel'– *because you don't!* Even if you have been through a similar experience yourself, you still do not know what someone else is going through or how someone else feels. Even though you meant well it may have the effect of making the other person angry or irritated.

You are also in danger of switching the spotlight from the speaker onto yourself – an added irritation! Think of an alternative and less presumptuous way of acknowledging their feelings. Try to do this by stating facts like: *'I can see that it's upsetting you a lot just to talk about it...', 'You really do sound unhappy with your present situation...', 'I can see the excitement in your eyes – I'm excited too!'* This is a far less contentious way of acknowledging the speaker's feelings and it greatly reduces the potential for causing irritation or taking away the spotlight.

Summarising

If you are listening to someone for any length of time it is possible to lose track of what is being said. It often helps to summarise what you think the speaker is saying at regular intervals. This has the double benefit of enabling you to check your understanding and at the same time it lets the speaker know that you are listening.

Using silence

How easy it is to forget that silence is one of the most powerful tools available to encourage people to talk!

Silence can make people feel awkward and consequently they often feel that they have to say something to break the silence. How many times have you found yourself being the one who breaks the silence?

Silence can be a salesman's most powerful tool if only he thinks to use it! By shutting up and listening to what his customer has to say he can learn so much about what his customer wants or needs.

> Silence is a vital part of listening actively. It gives the speaker time to think about what he is saying and it gives the listener time to think about what the speaker has said.

If the listener breaks the silence there is a danger that this will cause the speaker to *lose the moment* – forget what he was going to say, or prevent him from saying it.

Remaining silent allows you to listen, with empathy, to what the speaker does *not* say. Try to put yourself in the speaker's position and to understand the feelings he may be experiencing. Listen for clues to issues that are not being expressed. These could be verbal clues '*Yes, everything is* generally *okay at work*' or non-verbal clues – wringing hands nervously when talking about a particular person or place.

If appropriate, encourage or gently prompt the speaker to open up about these issues '*You said everything is* generally *okay...tell me more about what you mean by generally?*' But take care not to be persistent or put words into the speaker's mouth.

The following is a powerful example of the use of silence. It relates to a young lady who attended one of our courses. Something was very obviously troubling her and one of the trainers, with whom she had built up a trusting relationship, asked her if she would like to talk.

Case study

'I could see that Sharon was upset about something. Outwardly she was putting on an act, giving people the impression that she was a happy-go-lucky person who enjoyed going out for a drink with her friends. But whenever someone else talked about their past or about being happy she looked uneasy.

I took her to a quiet area and asked if it would help to talk. At first she was reluctant to say anything. I tried to gently encourage her to talk "I can see that something's upsetting you and if there's anything I can do to help then please tell me." I looked her in the eyes and remained silent. She was very uncomfortable looking at me – this was something that I had noticed earlier too when she spoke to anyone. I alternated my gaze between her and the floor. This seemed to relax her a little and she began to talk without me saying anything more.

Gradually she told me how she had been sexually abused as a child and how she had tried to wipe all of her childhood memories out of her mind. She resented listening to other people whose childhood had been happy. She knew that she needed professional counselling but had put off going to see her doctor to request a referral to a counsellor.

She talked for about an hour. I still felt that she had not told me everything that was troubling her, but this was a start. During that hour I spoke on only very few occasions, and then it was mainly to let her know that I could see how much it was upsetting her.

Later in the week she broke down during one of the sessions and I took her outside for a walk around the hotel grounds. We were there for almost two hours. During that time she told me much more detail about the abuse – it had been members of her close family, amongst others, who had abused her and she was still living with one of them.

There were times when neither of us spoke for five or ten minutes. These silences did not feel at all uncomfortable. It would have been totally inappropriate for me to break the silences – I could have destroyed her chance to talk by interrupting her train of thought. If she wanted me to say something, she asked. During the whole two hours I hardly said a word, but I *listened* very carefully to everything she said and I encouraged her to go on by nodding or saying 'Mmm . . .' to let her know that I was listening.

By listening I was able to pick up on one thing that seemed to be a potential silver lining to her clouded life. She made a comment "When I see children standing on street corners looking sad I wonder if they're being abused too. I want to go up to them and say *'If you want to talk to me about it I can help you – it happened to me too"*.' I asked her if she had ever thought about working with children who were victims of abuse. She hadn't, but her eyes lit up and she started to talk about how she believed that she could help them because of her own experiences.

By the end of the course she had made a decision to go and see her doctor to get referred for professional counselling to sort her own life out. She had also decided that she wanted to work with child abuse victims, and had resolved to enquire about studying and taking some qualifications in that field. She knew that she had to sort herself out first, but she seemed to have found the future that she thought could never be hers.

I would never have been able to help her if I hadn't just shut up and listened to her. That's how powerful silence and active listening can be. Sharon said she would be happy for me to relate her story to other people if it would help them to see that clouds *can* have silver linings'. _____

Behaviours to avoid for effective active listening

If when you are listening to someone, you find that you are guilty of any of the following behaviours, try to stop yourself. Think how much more effective you would be by making these small changes.

Interrupting or jumping in

You know the feeling, don't you? You're talking in full flow, concentrating pretty hard on what you're saying and then someone interrupts you. Or you're deep in thought and someone jumps in and says something. How does it make you feel? Angry? Irritated? Unimportant? Frustrated?

Apart from being incredibly rude, interrupting someone or jumping in to have your say can cause the moment to be lost and the speaker may never get around to saying what they wanted to say. It may also make the people you interrupt reluctant to trust you again because they think you are not really interested in them, only in trying to impose your views on them.

How often do you find yourself preparing your answer before the speaker has finished talking? Are you sure you always have the full picture? Why do you have to have your say? Remember to let the speaker finish before you say anything – that way you are more likely to have all the facts.

> It's often difficult not to interrupt someone who is speaking. We may have grown up seeing our peers and elders using this behaviour and think it's acceptable.

Can you honestly say that you never interrupt people? There is of course a time and a place – sometimes you need to interrupt someone in order to shut them up or to make a point, but when you are actively listening to someone you should try *not* to interrupt them.

Agreeing or disagreeing

Picture the scene. A woman is talking to a friend about an argument she had with her boyfriend. He often says he works late in the evenings but she suspects he is seeing another woman. She tells her friend that she intends to telephone her boyfriend and end their relationship and she asks her friend if she thinks that is the right thing to do. Her friend says yes so she goes ahead, reluctantly, and ends the relationship – after all, her friend agreed it was the right thing to do. She is then upset about giving her boyfriend the elbow.

She subsequently finds out that her now ex-boyfriend had not been seeing another woman – he really had been working late. Who do you think she's going to blame for ending the relationship? Herself or the friend who agreed that it was the right thing to do? The friend is unlikely to escape some of the blame.

> One of the key skills of active listening is to get the speaker to come to their own decision or conclusion.

You will not achieve this by agreeing or disagreeing with them because by doing that you are taking the responsibility for making the decision away from them.

So what should you do instead?

Try throwing the ball back into their court *'What do you think you should do?', 'Do you think that's the right thing to do?'* Refuse to be drawn into agreeing or disagreeing, instead help them to draw their own conclusion.

An effective way of doing this can be to ask them to weigh up the pros and cons, or advantages or disadvantages, of their proposed action. Encourage them to talk through alternative courses of action and to think about the pros and cons of these too. Remember, you are there to *listen* so make sure that the other person does the majority of the thinking and speaking. If there needs to be a long silence while they think then remember to remain silent – do not jump in and say something.

Giving advice

Firstly you need to understand that there are some situations where it is perfectly okay to give advice once you have listened to what the speaker has to say. For example if you are a sales person and you have listened to your customers explaining in detail what they want then, when you have all of the facts, you can advise them on the most suitable product to satisfy their needs. Or if you have listened to someone explain how they struggled to do something it is *sometimes* appropriate to give advice, but only if you honestly believe they will gain more from this than from discovering it for themselves.

In most other situations though this is similar to agreeing

or disagreeing with the speaker and the same rules apply. Even if you are asked for your advice you should try to get the speaker to find an appropriate solution. You may be asked things like:

♦ *'What would you do if you were in my situation?'*
♦ *'What do you think I should do?'*

Your response should be to encourage people to think for themselves, even if it means throwing the ball back into their court several times. Use questions like:

♦ *'What do you think you should do?'*
♦ *'What choices do you have?'*

If the response is *'I don't know'* then try using silence to get them to think about it for a while. If you get into the habit of providing solutions for other people they will always look to you, or to someone else, rather than making the effort to think up their own solutions.

Once again, think about this – if you give them advice and it all turns out wrong, who do you think they will blame, either wholly or partly?

Colouring or telling war stories

It is very likely that you know people who do this – who leap on the slightest cue to turn the conversation around to themselves and what *they* have done or where *they* have been. Maybe you've done it yourself too?

Colouring is picking up on something that someone says and then telling them how you did it better – you may not actually say *'I did it better'* but that's the gist of what you're saying. Here's an example of colouring:

'I've got tickets to see Bruce Springsteen in concert at the Royal Albert Hall in a couple of months time. I'm so excited.'

'Oh, I've got tickets to go and seem him too. My friend got them for me – she's a music journalist and she's arranged for me to go backstage and meet him afterwards too.'

That's colouring! It can be selfish and thoughtless and arrogant, to put it mildly! It smacks very much of one-upmanship. How do you think the other person feels when this happens? If you had it done to you, how would you feel?

There are, unfortunately, some people who do this all of the time. They are not interested in what you have to say other than as a springboard to embellish it with a story of their own.

Telling war stories is similar to colouring but it does not necessarily contain the element of *going one better* than the speaker. It still involves taking over the conversation and turning the spotlight on yourself, but to say '*I did that too*' or '*I did something similar to that*'. For example:

'*We just finished building our own house.*'

'*We built our own house too. It took us ages – we had to wait months before the plans got passed, and then the builder's merchant didn't have the bricks that we wanted...*'

What has happened in the above example is that the second person has taken over the conversation and stolen the first person's spotlight. It can be very annoying when someone does that to you.

If you think back to the anti-influential behaviours that you looked at in chapter three, you will probably agree that colouring or telling war stories should be added to the list. There are people who do that sort of thing all the time and don't even seem to realise that they're doing it. They enjoy turning the spotlight on themselves, but what they fail to see is the impact that their behaviour has on the people whose conversation they take over.

When you are actively listening to someone there is no place for colouring or telling war stories.

When to use active listening

So when should you use the skill of active listening? The simple answer is anywhere and any time that you desire good communication with another person. It can be extremely powerful in any of the following situations:

◆ To help you to build a good relationship at an early stage with new friends, acquaintances and work colleagues.

◆ To stop you from responding to, or arguing against, ideas or proposals that you have only half understood.
◆ To act as a sounding board and help people to clarify their own issues and arrive at their own solutions.

Let's look at each of these in more detail.

To help you to build a good relationship at an early stage with new friends, acquaintances and work colleagues

One of the best ways to get to know people is to encourage them to tell you about themselves – their background, their family, their interests and so on. This applies both in a social situation, with new friends or neighbours, and in a business or work situation with a new colleague or a new customer. This does not mean that you have to interrogate everyone you meet about every facet of their life, but simply that you can learn a lot by showing a genuine interest and *listening* to what they have to say.

Think about how good it makes you feel when someone takes a genuine interest in *you* – apart from anything else it helps you to warm to them more quickly and it also helps to build a good relationship from the start. It feels good when people remember little things that are important to you – like your children's names and birthdays, where you're going for your holiday this year, the fact that you enjoy going to the pictures. It feels good too when the greengrocer remembers that you prefer Granny Smith apples to Golden Delicious, or when the butcher remembers that you prefer a lean cut of meat. If you have to work away from home and stay in hotels a lot, it's nice when the receptionist remembers your name and that you prefer to have a room on the first floor. It makes you feel that you are important to that person and that they have actually listened actively to what you have told them.

By taking the time and trouble to listen to people you meet it gives you the opportunity to get to know them first hand rather than having to rely on someone else's opinion! Can you put your hand up and say that you've never formed an opinion of a person based on what someone else has told you 'Oh, him – *I could tell you a thing or two about* him . . .'? If you think about it, this is unfair and often does great injustice to a person. Far better to get to know someone yourself and form your own opinion.

In a work situation managers could learn so much about the people who work for them if they listened actively to them. They could find out what motivates them, what they enjoy about their work and what they don't enjoy, what their ambitions are and many more facts that can help to manage people effectively. If *you* have been in employment, how many of the managers that you worked for knew enough about you to know how to get the best out of you? When you come across such a manager – one who not only knows what motivates you at work but who also remembers details about your family and your interests and so on – there's a fair chance that you will enjoy working for this person and that you will remember him or her long after you work for them.

It's sad to hear people saying things like *'My manager can't even remember how many children I've got', 'It's my first day back from my holiday and my manager didn't bother to ask me if I'd had a nice time', 'I've just passed my exams but my manager didn't congratulate me'*. It's sad because it makes people feel that they are just another cog in the wheel and that they are not really important.

This applies equally to peers and colleagues. Active listening can be very influential and can help you command respect and loyalty because people see that you are someone who genuinely cares.

Listening actively to people, remembering what they tell you and using that information to make them feel important is a small courtesy that can pay huge dividends if only you can get into the habit of doing it. Recalling details of what you have previously been told can also be very influential.

To stop you from responding to, or arguing against, ideas or proposals that you have only half understood

Have you ever been in a situation where you have leapt into a conversation and argued against what someone was saying without fully understanding or hearing their point of view? As a simple illustration of this, imagine that you and your partner are talking about where to go on your holiday this year. Your partner suggests that you stay in this country. You want to go abroad, so you leap straight in and begin to argue against staying in this country before you have even heard your partner's reasons for suggesting it!

There are two points to consider here. The first is a very basic one – it is rude to jump in on what someone else is saying – even when that 'someone else' is your partner! Think back to the anti-influential behaviours that you looked at in chapter three and how you would feel if someone interrupted you without really listening to what you had to say. The likely outcome of this is an argument or a heated conversation that ends in stalemate because neither of you is really *listening* to what the other person has to say. Each of you is intent on putting your own point of view across.

The second point is that by jumping in you are making your response without fully understanding the other person's reasons for making the suggestion. Even though you may not initially like or agree with what the other person is saying, if you ask for their reasons it may help you to understand where they are coming from. For example, in the above situation instead of jumping in and saying that you want to go abroad you could simply ask your partner *'Why do you want to stay in this country?'* and *listen* to the reasons before responding. Make sure you find out all of the reasons. You may need to ask more questions, or point out things that your partner may not have considered like *'Have you thought about the weather – it's normally cold at that time of year?'* Your partner's reasons may be very good ones – like saving money so that you can have a really special holiday next year – but unless you ask and *listen* to the response you may never find out.

Even more important, when you have heard the reasons, weigh them up and adjust your own response accordingly. In other words, do not still leap in saying you think you should go abroad! *Acknowledge* what your partner has said – this shows that you really have been listening – and if you still disagree explain why and try to reach a compromise. For example, agree that it's a great idea to save money towards a special holiday next year, but explain that you'd really like to go somewhere to get sunshine and that's not very likely if you stay in this country. Offer a compromise: perhaps if you take your holiday in the summer rather than late autumn...

At work it is also important to listen to someone's reasons for suggesting something before making your response. If you do not agree with what they are saying, or if you do not understand it, ask them to explain their reasons. This will then give you the full picture on which you can base your response. This is far more constructive than just disagreeing with something because it doesn't initially sound like a good idea to *you*.

For example, if your manager asks you to work until seven o'clock on Friday evening to get an urgent order out your initial response might be you're not interested because you always go out on a Friday night. But there may be a good reason for asking you to do this – ask before making your response and *listen* to what your manager tells you. It may be that a new customer has placed a very large order that they want delivering by Saturday. If your Company can do this it stands to get repeat orders that will bring in a lot of money, which in turn will mean bonuses for all the work force. When you have the full details you can see that there's something in it for you and your colleagues – it may become a much more attractive proposition. Even if you still don't want to work late at least now you have all the facts on which to base your response and make alternative suggestions if appropriate – perhaps you wouldn't mind coming in earlier on Friday morning rather than staying late.

To act as a sounding board and help people to clarify their own issues and arrive at their own solutions

Skilful active listening can be enormously powerful in helping someone to talk through an issue that is concerning or troubling them. The issue could be a personal one, a family one, or a work one – anything at all that is giving someone cause for concern.

The case study on page 58 is a good example of using active listening to help someone clarify an issue that was troubling her and arrive at her own solution.

Sometimes someone will ask to talk to you, or there may be

times when you can see that someone has something on their mind and you may ask if they want to talk about it. Either way, your role will be to encourage them to talk, to *listen*, and then to encourage them to decide what they want to do. Remember what was said earlier about giving advice – in the majority of cases *don't*!

Try it now	Active listening is something that you can try straight away. Ask someone who you know well if you can listen to them. For your first attempt you may find it easier to ask a question about something you know they will be comfortable talking about. Explain why you want to listen to them and when they have finished talking, check the lists of behaviours you should and shouldn't do to see how you got on (there is a summary of these at the end of this chapter). By practising in a low-risk situation it should help you to build up your active listening skills.

Summary

Let's summarise what you have learned in this chapter about harnessing the power of influence. Firstly you looked at a technique that can help you to get rid of anti-influential behaviours:

Step 1

Think of a time when you displayed this anti-influential behaviour. Remember what you did and how you were feeling at that time.

Step 2

Think of an alternative and *positive* behaviour that you *could* have used.

Step 3

Ask yourself what made you choose the anti-influential, negative behaviour over the positive behaviour.

Step 4

Think about what you can do in future to ensure that you always choose to use the positive behaviour over the negative behaviour.

Next you looked at a similar technique that can help you to use more of the influential behaviours:

Step 1

Think of a time when you *could* have used an influential behaviour but you *didn't*. Remember what you did and how you were feeling at that time.

Step 2

Think about which anti-influential behaviour you *used* and which influential behaviour you could have used instead.

Step 3

Ask yourself what made you choose the anti-influential, negative behaviour over the positive behaviour.

Step 4

Think about what you can do in future to ensure that you always choose to use the positive behaviour over the negative behaviour.

And finally you looked at the power of being a good active listener. To help you do this effectively there is a list of behaviours you should use:

◆ Maintaining good eye contact.
◆ Clarifying a point.
◆ Asking questions *with care.*
◆ Acknowledging the speaker's feelings.
◆ Summarising.
◆ Using silence.

And a list of behaviours you should avoid:

◆ Interrupting or jumping in.
◆ Agreeing or disagreeing.
◆ Giving advice.
◆ Colouring or telling war stories.

You also learned that active listening can be used to good effect in the following situations:

◆ To help you to build a good relationship at an early stage with new friends, acquaintances and work colleagues.

- ◆ To stop you from responding to, or arguing against, ideas or proposals that you have only half understood.
- ◆ To act as a sounding board and help people to clarify their own issues and arrive at their own solutions.

All of the issues covered in this chapter are things that you can start working on straight away if you want to. The sooner you get into the habit of doing them, the more natural they will become.

CHAPTER 5

Putting the Past into Perspective

I cannot change yesterday, I can only make the most of today, and look forward with hope toward tomorrow.

C an you think of a time when someone hurt you or let you down, and the feeling caused you pain – emotional pain? How long did you suffer that pain? Perhaps you are still suffering with it years later. Think about what it does – or did – to you when you remember the event that caused the pain. Does it make you feel bitter, resentful, vengeful, sad, hurt, let down, unable to trust someone...? Did you ever consider forgiving the person who hurt you, or letting go of the past rather than constantly reminding yourself of the pain it caused you? Did you ever confront the person responsible for causing the pain in an attempt to resolve the issue?

Letting yourself down

Think also about any times when you have let *yourself* down – and consequently may have let other people down too. Perhaps you did a shoddy piece of work because you were bored or rushing; or maybe you went out for the evening with friends but didn't make any effort to join in the conversation because you were feeling unsociable. Maybe you sat around watching television all day instead of cleaning the house or weeding the garden or decorating the spare room. Perhaps you failed to stick to your diet, or start exercising.

> The effect of letting yourself down can be as painful as the effect of being let down by someone else. If you constantly let yourself down you may end up hating yourself, and if you hate yourself this can affect every aspect of your life – it certainly won't make you happy.

It is sad, the emotional pain that people inflict on each other, and on themselves. Sad because often it is avoidable. It is a very lucky, and rare, person who has never suffered any long-term emotional pain. Yet so much of it is unnecessary, because if the cause of the pain was dealt with at the time and then forgotten, the hurt and suffering could be short-lived rather than long-term.

Learning to forgive

It is not the intention of this book to examine in detail why people do what they do to each other – it is far too complex a subject to do justice to it here. However, the book will look at helping you prevent or deal with *emotional* pain and turn it to your advantage. Let's just put this into perspective. The pain we are talking about is the sort of emotional pain caused by someone else letting you down, betraying your trust, treating you badly, etc. It is not about *physical* pain or the sort of emotional pain you suffer when someone you love dies (we will look at ways to deal with the latter in the next chapter when we look at expressing feelings).

If you can learn to forgive people and let go of the past you can begin a healing process that will help you to develop and build a better future. For some people this will be much harder than others, particularly if they have been very badly let down. At this stage of the book you may not believe that it is possible to forgive and let go of the past – you may not want to. Take an extreme example like the Moors murders back in the 1960s where innocent children were tortured and killed, apparently for fun and sexual gratification. If you were the parent of one of the children who was killed, would you feel like forgiving or letting it go? And yet if you don't or can't it will nearly always be *you* who ends up suffering most because of holding it constantly in your consciousness and feeling the bitterness and resentment it can cause.

Understanding the difference between forgiveness and letting go

This is a good time to explain and clarify a few points about forgiveness and letting go. Firstly, please understand that forgiveness does not mean acknowledging that what was done was *right*. In fact it often entials admitting or acknowledging that it was *wrong*. But one thing is for certain, right or wrong *it cannot be undone* no matter how much you wish that it could. This is a true and logical fact. It may sometimes seem harsh, but it is correct. You literally cannot go back and change something that has already happened. Therefore it is logical to say that you can only go forward, having learned from any mistakes that were made. *How* you go forward is what this chapter will look at.

Secondly, for some people the pain of what has happened is so great they do not believe it is possible to forgive the person who caused the pain. If this is the case, the secret is to learn to let go of the past and all the pain and negative energy that accompanies it, because as long as you hold on to it you are keeping it in your consciousness and letting it drag you down. Focus instead on leaving it behind, acknowledging that you cannot change it, and moving on into the future. By doing this you will find that you can replace the negative energy with positive energy which can, in time, lead to forgiveness. Without forgiveness you will never truly be able to let go of the past. It will return to haunt you time and time again.

Understanding the difference between revenge and justice

When you have been wronged, or hurt, you may sometimes find yourself thinking about *revenge* – this is a certain indicator that you have not forgiven. It is important to point out here that revenge is not justice – even though you might like to think it is! Revenge and justice are two different things. Justice is the fair and legal way of dealing with a wrong-doing, whereas revenge implies a negative and sometimes illegal intent. However bad the deed that was done, two wrongs do not make a right.

> How many people have not felt the desire for revenge at some time in their life? Forgiveness and revenge do not make good bedfellows!

At the end of the day the path you follow is your choice but weigh up the long-term consequences very carefully. Forgiveness gives you an opportunity to let go and move on, revenge will often still be eating away at you years later – it can turn you into a very bitter person. The sad thing is that often this bitterness becomes so deep and natural that it changes your character. You may not be aware of how bitter you have become, but other people will see it in you. Bitterness is an anti-influential behaviour – remember the effect anti-influential behaviours can have.

Who suffers most?

Ask yourself this question: when you hang on to painful events from the past, who suffers the most? The chances are that *you do* and you may be making the people around you suffer too. Isn't it bad enough to suffer emotional pain because of what someone else has done? Why extend and prolong this by hanging on to it and refusing to forgive or let it go? Think about this point too: often the person who has wronged you or hurt you is not suffering at all and has effectively scored a *double whammy* over you – firstly by upsetting you, and secondly by seeing you prolong the suffering afterwards.

There are a growing number of people who believe that you can actually cause yourself physical illness – anything from a mild headache to a life-threatening cancer – by being bitter and resentful, and that forgiveness and letting go of the past can help to heal these ailments. Louise L Hay, a much respected writer in this field, has written books telling how she used forgiveness and letting go to help overcome her own life-threatening cancer and she cites numerous other cases of people it has helped. At the moment there is no scientific evidence to prove or disprove the theory, but there are a growing number of people who are convinced that it has helped them.

Remember the quote at the beginning of the chapter: '*I cannot change yesterday, I can only make the most of today, and look forward with hope toward tomorrow.* You are the only person who can prevent yourself from doing this, so it's up to you. Do you want the painful events of the past to stay with you, or do you want to leave them behind you and move on unburdened?

Case Study

'Kathy was my best friend when we were seventeen. We did everything together. Went to school, played truant, chased boys, went shopping and to the cinema, listened to music – she like Rod Stewart and I liked Elton John. She used to stay at my house, and I used to stay at hers. I thought the world of her, and I really enjoyed her company.

We even started going out with our boyfriends at the same time – they were brothers, John and Alan. My boyfriend, John, had a flash car which he used to take us all out in. He used to come and pick us up from school in it sometimes too, which we thought was great.

But Kathy wasn't really happy with Alan, and she finished with him. John introduced her to one of his workmates, Les, and soon we were going out again as a foursome. But soon she got fed up with Les too and ended the relationship.

She started to act a bit strangely with me, and make excuses about not going out. I tried to get John to introduce her to some more of his friends, but neither she nor he seemed interested. I though that perhaps she was jealous because I had a boyfriend with a nice car, and she didn't. Then she said she'd met someone else. By this time we had finished school, and we seemed to see less and less of each other. It was sad, but I had John, so I didn't really mind.

Then John started to act strangely with me. He started to accuse me of hiding information about my past from him. It didn't take me long to realise that it must be Kathy who was giving him this information because she was the only person who knew. He denied this, but my suspicions were roused.

One day I found a Rod Stewart cassette in his car. He never liked Rod Stewart but Kathy did. Several of my friends, including Alan and Les, told me that Kathy was going out with John behind my back – and had been all along. I confronted him about this, but again he denied it. I made myself believe him because I didn't want to contemplate my future without him, but in my heart I think I knew all along that he was lying.

I went out with John for almost four years before I discovered he was engaged to Kathy! And then I only found out because he broke down in front of me after she ended their engagement. All that time I'd deluded myself that he loved me. He swore that it was over and that he wanted to be with me, but for me the magic had gone. I hated Kathy with all my heart and soon came to hate John too. It was me that eventually ended our relationship.

I spent the next 15 years of my life hating them both and wishing I could get my revenge. At first I even thought about killing her or maiming her – I used to fantasise about it. I was very bitter, and vowed never to forgive them. I got married, but I still could not forgive and forget. I hoped that they were both as unhappy as they had made me.

One day, several years later, I saw John's sister at the cinema. She told me John and Kathy were married and had two very naughty, hyperactive children, and their marriage was not going well. She also told me that John's mum and the rest of the family had been very sad about what happened. They all missed me. I felt good. I was happy and they weren't, and they'd both got what they deserved – each other!

Slowly I began to realise that there was no point at all in continuing to hate them. I realised that I was wasting time and energy clinging on to something that had happened in the past, and nothing I could do – *nothing* – could change it. It had happened and it was physically impossible to undo it. I looked at the situation logically. *I* was the one who was suffering because by being so bitter about it I was keeping it in my consciousness. I had nothing to gain by holding on to the past, and everything to gain by letting go of it.

By continually repeating that logic to myself I eventually managed to let go of all my hatred. As part of the process I even telephoned Kathy and said I'd like to get together sometime – after all, we'd been best friends at one stage. She was very surprised to hear from me. Although we haven't actually got together yet, I felt so much better. We sent each other Christmas cards that year.

I no longer hate her – or him. In fact, I very rarely think about them, but when I do it is never with hatred or bitterness. I'm actually grateful for what happened because it helped to make me what I am today, and I'm proud of that. Looking back, I can't believe the energy I wasted over being bitter. I'm not sure what I thought it was going to achieve, but it certainly took a great chunk out of my life unnecessarily – and fruitlessly.' _____

Taking the first step to forgiveness

The following exercise can help you take the first step towards forgiving and letting go of the past. It requires you to think about all the people who have, at some stage in your life, caused you emotional pain – however great or small. People who, when you think about them, still cause you to feel emotional pain or resentment. The more you think about them, the greater your need to forgive and let go.

You may need to go right back to your childhood. As you grew up you might have found yourself living out other people's life scripts (what *they* wanted for you rather than what *you* really wanted for yourself) and consequently resenting them for making you do it. For example, perhaps you wore smart clothes because your *parents* wanted you to, although you would have preferred to wear jeans and trainers. Or you studied science at school because your *teacher* though you'd make a good biologist – and there was a shortage of biology graduates, but you would have preferred to study English Literature. Perhaps you had a wild party for your 21st birthday because your *friends* wanted you to, when really you would have preferred to have a small party at home. Maybe you didn't apply for a promotion at work because your *boss* didn't want to lose you, so you missed out on the opportunity of a job you would have really liked.

If anything that someone did in your past is still causing you pain or resentment, you need to forgive them for this and let go of it in order to move towards a better future.

Think also about all of the things *you* have done that have emotionally damaged other people, or something you're not proud of doing. These are things you need to forgive *yourself* for if you are to move towards a better future. It is as important to forgive yourself as it is to forgive others. If you can't forgive yourself you may end up hating yourself. Remember what we said earlier though – forgiving yourself does not mean acknowledging that what you did was *right*, because it may not have been. It means acknowledging that you cannot change it, but at the same time making sure you learn from it and don't repeat it.

To help you do this, think about why you acted as you did. Be very honest with yourself about it or you may find that you are hiding the real reason and this will not help you to deal with it.

Try it now

1. Make a list of all the things you need to forgive yourself for – things you are not proud of or things you have done that have caused pain to others. Try to remember *why* you did what you did.

   For example: *'I need to forgive myself for being spiteful to my younger brother when we were children. I know it was wrong, but I was very jealous of him. I had been an only child until he was born and I did not like it when he became the centre of attention.'*

2. Make a list of all the things that you need to forgive other people for (list these individually) – things they have done that have caused you pain or problems.

   For example: '*I need to forgive my father for giving all his love and attention to my new baby brother when he was born. It made me think my father didn't love me any more and that in turn made me jealous of my brother.*'

Once you have completed the above exercise you should find you are ready to move on to the process of forgiving and letting go of the past. Some people are able to do this simply by saying out loud '*I forgive you/myself unconditionally for...*' Go through your lists now and see if this works for you. Feel the forgiveness like a great weight lifting from your shoulders. Picture the resentment or pain disappearing over the horizon.

However, the majority of people need a little more help to forgive and let go. If you fall into this category, the techniques discussed below will help you.

Writing a truth letter

A very powerful procedure that has helped many people to forgive others and to let go of the past is writing a truth letter. This is a letter in which you express all of your feelings – positive and negative – to a person who you need to forgive. Someone who has caused you emotional pain, or who you feel has been responsible in some way for making you the way you are. You may find that you need to write several letters to different people in order to benefit fully.

The letter should never be posted, it is the physical *process* of writing the letter that is important – getting in touch with and expressing your feelings. Indeed the person to whom you write the letter may be dead so it would not be possible to post it, but it is still important to express the feelings in order to let them go.

The first of your truth letters might be to your parents (individually), thanking them in detail for all the good things they did for you, but also expressing your feelings about other things they did that were not good or that have caused you problems in later life, even though they may have been well intentioned.

Once you have done the truth letters to your parents, you should think about all the other people in your life (currently, and in the past if you are still holding on to past resentments). Refer to the list that you made of people you need to forgive. Would writing a truth letter to any of them help you to forgive them and let go of the past?

The format for writing a truth letter is simple:

1. Begin by writing the person's name, as you would when writing a normal letter: '*Dear...*'

2. Thank them for all of the good things they did for you: '*I thank you for...*' It is important to list each of these things individually. Do not just say '*Thank you for all of the good things you did for me*'. By detailing the things individually it helps you to get in touch with them better and acknowledge them for what they are worth.

3. Write down all of the things you do not thank them for – the things you believe have caused you pain or problems, no matter how small or large: '*I do not thank you for...*' Once again, remember to detail each thing individually and try to say why it caused you pain.

4. Sign your name in an appropriate way: '*From...*', '*Love from...*', '*Yours...*', but *never* with resentment or sarcasm as this indicates forgiveness has still not taken place.

In a moment you will see some examples of truth letters, but first there is an important point to make. The purpose of a truth letter is to help you forgive someone or let go of the past. In order to do that effectively it is necessary to remember and express all of the negative feelings you have about the person to whom the letter is written. Please do not confuse this with moaning, blaming others, playing victim, or any of the other anti-influential behaviours that you looked at in chapter three. This is something you do in private, and for nobody else but yourself to see.

> The great thing about the truth letter is that it should actually prevent you from displaying any of those behaviours publicly because you have already dealt with them in private.

The process of writing the truth letter has helped you to bring them to the forefront of your consciousness, acknowledge them and express your pain or anger. Only by doing this can you ever hope to get rid of those feelings and forgive the person and let go of the past.

As a result of writing a truth letter you may feel motivated to talk to the person concerned. Before you do this, think very carefully about the impact this might have – will they understand what you are saying, and why? A truth letter is a very personal thing. Take care not to stir up a hornet's nest and end up making the situation worse. If the truth letter has worked for you, and the forgiveness has taken place, there is *normally* no need to talk to the other person about it. If you still feel it is appropriate to talk to the other person, do it constructively, never blaming them or showing resentment.

Figures 1 and 2 on page 81 and 82 are examples of how a truth letter might look. These are abridged examples for the purpose of demonstrating the technique – a full truth letter may need to go on for much longer. One is to a parent, the other is based on the case study on page 75, to a friend who caused pain.

Don't worry if you don't get around to finishing your truth letters, so long as they have helped you to forgive and let go of the past. Some people never get around to finishing their truth letters because they find that they are able to forgive and let go part way through the process. Some people keep them locked away, or tear them up, or burn them because this makes them feel better. The important thing is to enjoy the benefits a truth letter can confer, as Graham (a sales manager) in the case study explains.

Case Study

'When I wrote my truth letter to my parents I found that although there was a lot of pain and upset to re-live and re-visit, I got a lot of positive messages and a feeling of understanding my parents in a way I never did before. I realised that there was no malicious intent to upset or deny me, rather two people who tried to live their own lives as well as bring up two kids *as they saw fit*.

I recognised their individual competitiveness to get ahead – a trait which is fundamental in my own success. Their willingness to please and their efforts not to upset people through denying them – even though that is always what

Dear Mum,

I thank you for bringing me into this world and caring for me until I was old enough to look after myself. You taught me, by your own example, to be kind and considerate to other people and to be unselfish. You taught me that there are more important things in life than money. All of these things I have come to understand and appreciate more as I have grown older.

Thank you for believing in me and encouraging me to follow my dreams, even when everyone else thought I was crazy. You shared my vision of the dream home that I was going to create, and you always believed that I could succeed at whatever I did. You were right, and I thank you for your belief.

I do not thank you for repressing your feelings – you did so many little things that made me *think* you loved me and that I was special to you, but Mum, you rarely told me you loved me and that would have meant so much to me. I only remember you telling me twice. Once when we hadn't been speaking to each other for weeks because we'd had an argument and once just before you died. If you had let me know you loved me when I was a child I may not have grown up thinking you loved my brothers more. This made me jealous because I never knew how you felt about me. I felt I had to compete for your love and I was never sure if I'd won. Because I grew up without being encouraged to express my love I now find it very difficult to tell people close to me that I love them – it doesn't feel like a normal thing to do.

I do not thank you for being unassertive, particularly with dad. You always seemed to be afraid of him and because of that you never stood up to him, even if you disagreed with him. You used to back down in order to keep the peace – not just with Dad, but with lots of people. Consequently I grew up to be unassertive myself and ended up backing down to people, or saying the right thing in order to keep the peace. This has caused me a lot of pain in my life. The only way I knew of being assertive was to get angry and shout – because that's what Dad used to do.

Love from...

Fig. 1. Example of a truth letter.

Dear Kathy,

Thank you for being my friend at school and for all the fun we had together. I enjoyed being with you because we were so alike and we used to like the same things except that is, Rod Stewart and Elton John. You know, I actually enjoy Rod's music now. I particularly used to enjoy going shopping in our lunch hours and trying on all the latest fashions, although we could never afford to buy anything.

Thank you for inviting me to stay at your parents' house – I used to enjoy talking and listening to records and reading pop music magazines together. I especially used to enjoy getting a Chinese take-away. It was a real treat for me because I only had a fish and chip shop where I lived.

This may sound strange, but I really do thank you for marrying John. With the benefit of hindsight I can see that he was totally wrong for me and if you hadn't done what you did I might have ended up marrying him myself and missing out on the wonderful life that I now have. So, in a roundabout way you actually did me a huge favour. I'm sad for you in some ways, because I know that he has been unfaithful to you on more than one occasion since you got married. Once I used to think it was good that you got a taste of your own medicine but now I just feel sad for you.

However, I do not thank you for going out with John behind my back. I can understand why you fancied him because I did too, but it was a cruel and deceitful thing to do to me. It made me mistrustful of many other people who I subsequently met, because your behaviour made me think everyone was untrustworthy, especially women. To this day I still have very few women friends. That took me many years to get over, and even now I sometimes find myself mistrusting people's motives.

I do not thank you for betraying my confidence by telling John about things that happened in my past – former boyfriends who you knew he did not like. You tried to make him think that I had lied to him in the hope that he would end our relationship and that caused me an enormous amount of pain at the time. It also made me reluctant to divulge details about my past to other people in case they too used them to hurt me. I used to be suspicious whenever anyone asked me about my past because I though they would use it to hurt me, so I became very defensive and secretive. I often made things up because it seemed easier that way.

From. . . .

Fig. 2. Example of a truth letter.

seemed to happen and their own parents' influence on what they did and what they tried to live up to.

The most important thing that the truth letter did for me was to release all my frustrations, bitterness and ill-feeling and replace them with understanding, sympathy and a willingness to help others overcome their own demons. The truth letter helped me to realise that my parents are in fact two people who, like the rest of us, are not perfect but need a little help along the way. I only wish they could have had the benefit of the truth letter – not for my sake as their child, because they made me what I am and I'm very happy with my life – but for their own benefit so that they too could be content with their lives.'

> The truth letter helps you to leave the past behind and move unencumbered into the future.

By leaving the past behind you can channel your energy in a positive direction. Part of this process involves learning from your mistakes – and other people's.

Learning from your mistakes

Almost every book that you read about people who have made it to the top of their profession will tell how they have made mistakes on the way. The important point is that they have always learned from these mistakes and this has helped them to develop and go forward. In doing this they have turned a negative situation into a positive one.

An important part of building a new future is learning to accept that *everybody* makes mistakes, yourself included. The word mistake means *error* or *slip* – in other words it is something unintentional, unplanned. There is little point in punishing yourself, or anyone else, for making a genuine mistake because once it has been made it is impossible to undo it. Only when you fully understand and accept this can you learn to forgive other people – and yourself – for making mistakes, no matter how serious the consequences.

So, accepting that people make mistakes is the first step to treating it positively rather than negatively. Dealing with the mistake is the next step – learning from it in order to prevent it from happening again. The following process is particularly useful for helping you to do this:

Step 1. Find out why the mistake happened. For example, was it because of carelessness, laziness, not understanding how to do something, unclear instructions, etc. Only by understanding why it happened can you hope to prevent it from happening again. If it was your fault, accept responsibility – do not try to blame someone else.

Step 2. Assess what you need to do differently to make sure it does not happen again.

Step 3. Take positive action to ensure that it does not happen again. If appropriate, make sure you inform other people too so they do not make the same mistake.

Example

You decide to write to the local branch of your bank to enquire if they have any job vacancies. You address your letter to *Mr C. Cross, The Manager...*' because you have seen the name C. Cross written on the door of the manager's office. However, what you do not realise is that C. Cross is a *female* bank manager.

You have made a mistake which could potentially affect the outcome of your job enquiry. So, apply the above technique:

Step 1. Find out why the mistake happened

The mistake happened because you assumed that C. Cross was a male bank manager. You did not bother to check on this before sending off your letter. If you had bothered to check you would have discovered two useful facts. Firstly that C. Cross was female, and secondly that all job applications should be sent to the bank's regional office.

Accept responsibility for your mistake. Do not try to blame someone else for failing to give you the correct information.

Step 2. Assess what you need to do differently to make sure it does not happen again

You need to check before sending out a job application that

you have got all the details correct. Getting them wrong creates a bad first impression – you may not get a second chance! Never make assumptions or guesses.

Step 3. Take positive action to ensure that it does not happen again

Make a checklist of all the things you need to do before sending off any more job applications. Check the name – including the correct spelling – of the person to whom your application should be sent. Check the address – including the correct spelling – to which your application should be sent. If you are not sure of all the things you need to do, speak to someone who can help you.

Having made the checklist, ensure that you follow it! And if you know someone else who is applying for a job, show them the checklist too so they can benefit from what you have learned.

Try it now Think about a mistake that you made in the past, where you reacted in a negative way or you did not deal with it at the time. Follow the above process in order to learn something positive from the mistake.

Next time you make a mistake, follow the process as soon as you possibly can.

By focusing your energy on making sure it does not happen again you are not only taking positive action, but you are also avoiding falling into the trap of feeling sorry for yourself. All too often, especially if you are feeling down, it is easy to focus on the negative things that have happened to you and to blame other people: *'If only someone had told me...'* Try instead to focus on learning from the mistake, and encourage other people to do likewise.

Learning to value yourself

Once you have discovered the power of forgiveness and letting go of the past, you are ready to focus on the present, on learning to value yourself.

Valuing yourself is about acknowledging that you are important and that you deserve to have a successful and happy life. If you do not believe this, you cannot expect to achieve it.

The biggest problem with most people is that they do not value themselves enough. This causes them to have low self-esteem and to doubt themselves and their worth. Below are listed just a few of the negative consequences that can result from not valuing yourself enough:

◆ You let other people have their way or walk all over you.

◆ You are submissive because you find it difficult to stand up for yourself.

◆ You are aggressive because you think that shouting and getting angry is the only way to get other people to take any notice of you.

◆ You have a problem being assertive or saying *No* to anyone because you think people won't like you if you say you are unable or unwilling to help.

◆ You tend to be negative and moan about things because you think other people have got something better than you, or they have taken advantage of you, etc.

◆ You make excuses or tell white lies rather than telling the truth because you are afraid you will upset or offend people.

◆ You doubt yourself and your abilities, which leads you to see the negative side of things *'He didn't ask me to ... because he thinks I'm not good enough'*.

◆ You find it hard to take criticism because you think it is an attack on your personality not your behaviour – and because of this you often become defensive.

◆ You believe you are not as good as other people. This can lead to missing out on many things that you want, from personal relationships *'She'd never go out with me'* to a better job *'I wouldn't stand a chance'*. It can also mean you see other people as a threat.

◆ You get stressed easily as a result of some or all of the above.

However, once you learn to value yourself you will find that the pay-offs are enormous. Valuing yourself is the key to unlocking so many doors that you may otherwise have believed to be closed. Below are just some of the many benefits that come from valuing yourself

◆ You have a positive outlook and see the good in people and things.

- You stand up for what you believe in, even if it means upsetting other people.
- You find it easy to be assertive because you believe that your opinion is as valuable as anyone else's.
- You remain calm, even under pressure, because you do not believe you have to shout and be aggressive to make your point.
- You do not have a problem saying *No* to anyone because you believe that you have the right to say it.
- You believe in yourself and your abilities, which leads you to persevere when necessary until you succeed (Walt Disney visited over 400 banks before he found one that would lend him the money to finance his dream – Disney World).
- You accept criticism and learn from it. You do not become defensive.
- You do not worry about making people like you because you accept that you cannot please all of the people all of the time. This enables you to speak your mind rather than say what you think other people want to hear.
- You rarely get stressed. When you do, you know how to handle it.

In learning to value yourself it is important to realise that your life is every bit as worthy as anyone else's. As you are the only person in your life over whom you have *total* control, this alone makes it important that you value yourself. You have this control because you, and you alone, have a choice of how to act in any given situation. Other people may have an *influence* (good or bad), but only you have *control.*

By valuing yourself you will believe, for example, that you have the right to say *No* and that you have as much right to hold and express your opinion as anyone else does. If you do not value yourself you may find yourself regularly putting other people and their needs in front of yours. This can cause you to have low self-esteem because you constantly feel that you are playing a passive role, reacting to other people's wants and needs rather than attending to your own. Let's just clarify a point here before moving on. We're talking about putting yourself and your needs first in a *rational* way – not a *selfish* way. A rational person says *'I'm sorry but I won't be able to help you decorate your front room this weekend because I've already made other plans.'* He doesn't feel bad about saying this because it is true, neither does he feel the obligation to explain exactly what his other plans are. A selfish person says *'No way, do it yourself! I've got better things to do.'* And the person who doesn't value himself enough says *'Oh, okay...'* and then suffers internally, or moans to someone else about it!

> By valuing yourself you are acknowledging that you have rights, and that your needs are as important as other peoples.

Recognising the importance of your own needs is very different to being selfish, where you act as though you are the only one who matters and your needs are *more* important than those of other people. Can you see the difference?

Valuing yourself also means that you will respect yourself, which in turn will raise your self-esteem. To put this into context, think about the difference between someone you respect and someone you do not. How do you act differently with someone you respect? Whose company do you prefer – the person you respect or the one you don't? Now relate this to *yourself* and think about the benefits to be gained when you respect *yourself* and the disadvantages and consequences of not respecting yourself.

Try it now In your notebook make a list of all your good qualities – things you believe you do to make a valuable contribution. For example *'I am a good father to my children because I love them and always try to understand and help them.'*
Keep this list somewhere that you can look at it often, to remind you of the valuable contributions you make. Add to it as you think of more things. Most of all, believe in it and be proud of it.

Learning to love yourself

So far in this chapter you have learned about the role that forgiveness, letting go of the past, and valuing yourself play in helping to have a better life. These three things are a prerequisite to loving yourself. You can only learn to love yourself once you:

◆ Forgive yourself and any person who has hurt you.
◆ Let go of the past.
◆ Value yourself properly and respect yourself.

> Loving yourself is not about being vain and egotistical. It is about appreciating all the good things about yourself.

You may find that you need to make some changes before you can love yourself. Think back to the work you have done so far in this book and the changes you have identified you need to make. In acknowledging that you need to make changes you are simply recognising that at the moment you do not like some of the things that you do or don't do. Therefore, until you make these changes there will still be things about yourself that you do not like.

Loving yourself is another vital step in choosing a better life. Why? Because when you love yourself:

◆ You are not damaged (emotionally) by what other people do or say.
◆ You can live on your own 'nourishment' without constantly needing praise or acceptance from other people.
◆ You can deal with issues without the need to play victim in an attempt to get sympathy.
◆ You happily take responsibility for making things happen.

Ask yourself the question *if you do not love yourself, why should other people love you?* If you do not love yourself you are saying – consciously or subconsciously – that there is something unlovable about you, so you should not be surprised if you find that other people do not love you either. Surely this alone is a good enough reason to seek out and deal with the unlovable elements of your character?

Try it now

1. In your notebook, write down all of the things that stop you from loving yourself. In other words, what would you have to change about yourself before you could love yourself?

2. What, if anything, is stopping you from making these changes?

3. Select *one* of the things you said you need to change and start work on it straight away. Begin by thinking about the disadvantages and consequences of *not* changing, then weigh these up against the advantages and benefits of *changing.*

You will do more work on learning to value yourself and love yourself as you progress though this book, however now is a good time to begin the process. Don't feel that you have to stop at dealing with just one thing you need to change. Please work on as many as you feel able to at this stage. The sooner you begin the sooner you will reap the rewards.

Summary

In this chapter you have learned a number of steps you need to take in order to prevent the past from having a negative impact on you, and thus holding you back from choosing a better life.

- ◆ The power of forgiveness and letting go of the past.
- ◆ Writing a truth letter.
- ◆ Learning from your mistakes.
- ◆ Valuing and respecting yourself.
- ◆ Learning to love yourself.

We nurse a
fiction that
people love to
cover up their
feelings.
DAVID GRAYSON

CHAPTER 6

Expressing Feelings

W hy is it so important to express your feelings and why
do you need to be able to do this if you are to have a
better life? The simple answer is that by expressing your
feelings you are letting other people know:

◆ How you feel about *them* – or their words or actions.
or
◆ How they have made *you* feel – with their words and actions.

> '*We nurse a fiction that people love to cover up their feelings;
> but I have learned that if the feeling is real and deep, they
> love far better to find a way to uncover it.*'
>
> *David Grayson*

Unless you let people know where they stand – and unless you
know where you stand – you or they will not have an
opportunity to react in an appropriate way. For example, if
someone knows that they have upset you – and *why* – they can
respond accordingly. But if you do not express your feelings or
let them know how they have upset you, they will not get the
true picture and thus they may respond inappropriately or not
at all.

Expressing your feelings is also in keeping with the six
principles for building a better life that you learned about in
Chapter 2.

◆ Be honest and open.
◆ Trust and be trustworthy.
◆ Give people descriptive feedback to help them develop.
◆ Be aware of any discrepancy between your impact and your
intention.
◆ Avoid being critical and judgmental about other people.
◆ Deal with issues before they become hidden agendas.

Ask yourself how good *you* are at expressing your feelings. Are you better at expressing feelings about some issues than others – for example, maybe you find it easy to express anger, but difficult to express love? Are there some people to whom you generally find it easy to express all of your feelings and others to whom you struggle to express any feelings? Is there one (or more) feeling that you find particularly difficult to express? By the time you get to the end of this chapter you should have a much clearer understanding of the benefits of expressing feelings and also why some people find it difficult to express certain feelings to certain other people.

Try it now

Taking each of the following feelings in turn think about how easy, or how difficult, you find it to express these feelings to the various people in your life. For example, you might find it easy to express anger to your children, but difficult to express anger to your neighbour who plays loud music late into the night. In your notebook write down each of these feelings (and any others you wish to add). As you write down each feeling, make two lists alongside it: 1. Those people to whom you find it *easy* to express the feeling. 2. Those people to whom you find it *difficult* to express the feeling. See if there are any patterns emerging, for example, are there some people to whom you easily express *all* feelings and others to whom you only find it easy to express *some* feelings? Is there one or more particular feeling(s) you find it easy or difficult to express to everybody?

- ◆ Love
- ◆ Affection
- ◆ Happiness
- ◆ Pride
- ◆ Grief
- ◆ Unhappiness
- ◆ Worry
- ◆ Anger
- ◆ Displeasure
- ◆ Doubt

How effectively do you express your feelings?

How *effectively* do you think you express your feelings? For example, if you find it easy to express anger, do you express it constructively *'I feel really angry about the way you treated me because...'* or do you tend to blow your top or fly off the handle *'What the hell do you think you're doing...'*. The way you express your feelings is likely to have a strong influence on the response you get. To put this into perspective think back to the influential and anti-influential behaviours you looked at in chapter three.

> If you express your feelings in an assertive way you are likely to have a far greater influence than if you express them in an aggressive way.

Think about the sort of response you get when you express your feelings – is it the one you would like? If not, this chapter will help you to examine why not. Only by understanding this will you be able to do something about it.

Are you active or passive?

Are you the sort of person who *actively* seeks to express your feelings? For example, do you tell your partner how much you love him or her, and why? Or are you *passive* when it comes to expressing your feelings? Do you keep your feelings to yourself or only express them in response to being asked how you feel *'Of course I love you...'*, *'Well, yes, I am a bit annoyed about it...'*?

Many people find it difficult to actively express their feelings whilst some find it only too easy, but fail to do it constructively! Often they are *in touch* internally with the way they feel about things, but when asked to *express* their feelings they can't. This can result in them being labelled cold or hard or unemotional by other people. Remember what we said in chapter two about the difference between your intention and your impact. People who find it difficult to express their feelings can very often have a totally different impact to their intention – they don't *intend* to be cold, or hard, or unemotional, but that can be the impression they create. This in turn can make them anti-influential which, as you have seen, could create its own set of problems.

Understanding conditioning

You have already learned how conditioning can affect the way people behave. It should be no surprise to learn that conditioning can also play a large part in influencing your ability to express your feelings. If you are brought up by parents who tell you that *'Big men don't cry'* and who believe it is a weakness to show your feelings, then that is likely to be the belief that you adopt yourself. These beliefs are often shared and supported by many other people who have an influence on you – teachers, friends, colleagues at work – many of whom have been conditioned this way too.

Exploring other influences

There are many other factors that influence how easy or difficult it is for you to express your feelings. It is likely that you will be able to do it more easily if you have experienced warmth, encouragement, and openness, for example if:

◆ Your parents often told you they loved you.
◆ Your parents and teachers praised you when you did things well and encouraged you to be proud of your achievements.
◆ Your parents and teachers taught you to accept responsibility for your actions – whether they resulted in success or failure – and to learn from your mistakes.
◆ Your partner often tells you that he or she loves you, and backs this up by the way he or she behaves.
◆ Your boss at work gives you praise when it is due and encourages and supports your development – which includes helping you to learn from any mistakes you make.
◆ Your boss at work is open and honest with you, even in difficult matters.
◆ Your colleagues at work show a real team spirit, and help and encourage each other for the success of the team.
◆ Your friends offer genuine, unselfish friendship and you are open and honest with each other.

If, on the other hand, your experience has been more negative you may be more likely to suppress your feelings, or express them inadequately or ineffectively, for example, if:

◆ Your parents rarely, if ever, told you they loved you.
◆ Your parents and teachers rarely, if ever, praised you when you

did things well and frequently criticised you when you did things wrong or badly. Your school report was full of *could do better*, but nobody seemed interested in helping you to improve.

◆ Your parents, teachers, friends and colleagues blamed other people when things went wrong, rather than accepting responsibility for their actions and learning from their mistakes.

◆ Your partner rarely, if ever, tells you that he or she loves you.

◆ A former or current partner has taken advantage of your feelings, or betrayed your trust.

◆ Your boss at work frequently criticises you and finds fault with your work, but rarely gives you praise or encouragement.

◆ Your boss at work is secretive, or tells lies or is economical with the truth.

◆ Your colleagues at work mistrust each other and are often competing against each other. There is very little, if any, team spirit.

◆ Your friends are selfish and use you because they think you are a soft touch.

◆ Your friends or family laugh at you if you cry at a sad film, or television programme, or if you appear to be generally emotional.

Why do people suppress their feelings?

How do new born babies know how to express their feelings from the day they are born? They cannot speak, so they show their feelings in other ways. If they are happy, they laugh or smile, and if they are in pain or want something, they cry or scream. All of us, as babies, express our feelings freely.

> It is only when children go through the process of growing up and are influenced by parents, teachers, workmates, friends, etc. that they begin to have problems expressing their feelings.

Children can be held back even further if they have been ridiculed or put down for expressing their feelings like *'Don't be so stupid'*, *'If that's how you feel there's nothing more to say'*, *'Don't let your father see you crying like that'*.

Wearing a mask

Even at work you cannot escape being in an environment where the suppression of feelings is widespread. Many companies are run on the premise that it is a weakness to show your true feelings, thus many of the people who work in such organisations find themselves wearing a mask – the *me at work* mask. Many, many people wear such a mask and suffer because of it. They suffer because they are trying to be two people. It is tough enough for them trying to value themselves, to have confidence, to have high self-esteem, to have a loving relationship, to make decisions, to have a happy life, to choose where to live and so on if they are *one person* – by putting on this *work mask* they are doubling the difficulty! Some of them even put on a *home mask* too so it becomes a three-way struggle between *the real me, the home mask* and *the work mask.* And they wonder why they suffer from stress – and confusion!

Carrying emotional baggage

Being in an environment where it is considered weak to show your true feelings – whether this is at home, at work, or socially – leads many people to suppress their feelings. So does being hurt, for example, in a relationship. People who have been hurt in a relationship often fear that if they show their feelings again they will get hurt again, so they suppress their feelings and as a consequence they hurt in a different sort of way.

But still the pain is there. The sort of pain that is normally much worse in the mind than in reality. The pain people carry inside which can often build up to form emotional baggage. They carry this baggage with them and it can affect the decisions they make in their dealings with other people. Such decisions are often made based on bad or painful experiences from the past – a past that they cannot change no matter how much they would like to.

The danger of carrying emotional baggage

Think about the disadvantages and consequences of not expressing your feelings. If you suppress your feelings they are locked away and can build up into emotional baggage that you will have to carry around with you. That baggage can get heavy. The build-up of baggage can become so great that it can explode, either when you are at a low point in your life – like when you are not feeling well – or when you are on a high – like when you fall in love with someone new. You can become confused by the emotions that you experience because of the build-up of suppressed feeling over many months or years.

The effect of the emotional build-up is like an active volcano – the pressure builds up over many years until – *pow* – it finally explodes! And when it explodes, many people can get hurt. Below is an example of how it can explode is when someone is on a high. The events and feelings are described with the possible reason for the emotional baggage that is being carried in brackets.

Example

A woman meets a man and they start going out with each other. She feels an enormous amount of love and passion in this new relationship and is on a high most of the time, but she also feels many other emotions which she doesn't understand.

♦ She feels *hurt* when her new boyfriend phones to rearrange a date (because she has been let down in the past by boyfriends who had lied to her and betrayed her trust).

♦ She is *suspicious* and *jealous* when she sees her new boyfriend talking to another woman at the station (because she has been two-timed in the past by previous boyfriends).

♦ She feels *guilty* when she has to work late one Friday evening and offers copious explanations and apologies to her new boyfriend (because one of her previous boyfriends was jealous and didn't trust her so she always had to prove what she said was true).

♦ She feels *angry* when her new boyfriend accuses her (jokingly) of being *a hard woman* when they go to the pictures because she doesn't cry at the sad ending (because a former boyfriend had accused her of being soft and causing him embarrassment when she cried at the end of another sad film).

♦ She feels *embarrassed* and blushes furiously, when he tells her she is beautiful – she's not sure if he means it or if he's joking

and consequently she misses the full enjoyment of the
compliment (because nobody has ever paid her such a
compliment before, unless sarcastically or tongue-in-cheek).

A self-fulfilling negative prophecy

Sometimes the confusion caused by the pressure of the built-
up emotions can result in totally irrational behaviour. In the
above example the girl might suddenly end the relationship for
no apparent reason, or because she can't believe her new
boyfriend is not going to turn out to be a *bad apple* just like
all her previous boyfriends. She may even end up unwittingly
engineering it so that her boyfriend ends the relationship
because he is so fed up with her irrational behaviour. She then
thinks *I knew he would be the same as all the others!* In other
words – it becomes a self-fulfilling negative prophecy.

It is so sad when something like this happens, because it
causes unnecessary suffering and pain – often to more than
one person. It is even sadder because, in the majority of cases,
it is preventable if only you can learn to express your feelings
appropriately.

Expressing your feelings more easily

Let's look at what you can do to help you express your feelings
with greater ease. First, consider some of the advantages of
being able to express your feelings.

♦ People know where they stand because they know how you feel
  about them, their words or their actions.

♦ You can be yourself because you don't have to wear a mask to
  hide or disguise your feelings.

♦ You are far more influential because you don't carry any
  emotional baggage that can make you act irrationally.

♦ You rarely suffer from stress or depression because you don't
  internalise your feelings by keeping them to yourself.

♦ You find it much easier to talk about painful events from your
  past, like the death of a loved one, because you are in touch
  with your feelings.

♦ You are not embarrassed to cry if you are upset – whether it is
  at a funeral or a sad film.

Now let's look at some of the disadvantages of not being able
to express your feelings:

◆ People don't know where they stand with you because they
  don't know what you are really thinking.

◆ People can get the impression that you are cold, hard or
  unfeeling, which can have an anti-influential effect.

◆ You often have to put on an act to disguise your true feelings
  so the real you remains hidden from view. You may find
  yourself thinking that people don't understand you.

◆ You often suffer from stress, and possibly depression.

◆ You deny yourself the opportunity to benefit from other
  people's help or advice because if you are unable to express
  how you feel they won't know if anything is wrong.

◆ You carry emotional baggage with you which can cloud your
  judgment and make you act irrationally in certain situations.

◆ As a consequence of not being able to express your feelings you
  often feel jealous, envious or guilty (more about this later).

So apart from understanding the advantages and disadvantages
of expressing, or suppressing, your feelings, what else can you
do that will help you feel at ease with expressing your feelings?
The following process should help.

Step 1. Discover the source of your discomfort

Think back to your past – you may have to go right back to
your childhood – and try to pinpoint what happened to make
you feel uneasy about expressing a particular feeling. For
example, if you find it difficult to tell people close to you that
you love them perhaps it is because your parents never used to
tell you that they loved you.

If you cannot think of anything, or cannot remember much
about your childhood, you might want to ask someone else if
they can help – your parents, an older brother or sister, an
aunt or uncle or a family friend.

If you really can't think of anything, don't worry about it!
You may find that something comes to you later, especially
now that you have brought it into your consciousness.

Step 2. List the disadvantages and possible consequences of not expressing this feeling

This list can be written down or simply done in your head – the important thing is to think very carefully about all of the disadvantages and possible consequences of not being able to express this feeling.

For example, if you cannot easily express your love to your partner then one of the *disadvantages* is that he or she will not know that you love him or her and may even think that you don't have any feelings for him or her at all (this is especially likely to happen if your partner suffers from low self-esteem and lack of confidence). A possible *consequence* is that your partner may seek love elsewhere by having an affair or leave you for someone else – or may even think that you are being unfaithful too!

Step 3. List the advantages and likely outcomes of expressing this feeling

Again, this list can be written down or simply done in your head – the important thing is to think very carefully about all of the advantages and likely outcomes of expressing this feeling.

For example, one *advantage* of telling your partner that you love her is that she will know how you feel. A likely outcome of this is that it will make your partner feel secure and less likely to seek love elsewhere.

> Remember that once you have expressed your feelings verbally your actions will need to support your words.

Once you have used this process to help you discover why you have a problem expressing certain feelings, think about how you can express your feelings more effectively in future – what sort of things can you say to make them sound genuine and be effective? It may take people by surprise if you just blurt out your feelings so think carefully about this before you open your mouth. There would be nothing worse than finding the courage to say what you feel then being laughed at or shot down in flames because you hadn't really thought about how you were going to do this.

You may feel it appropriate to begin by explaining that you don't normally say much about how you feel but you'd like to change that. If you need to express feelings of anger, or displeasure, remember what you learned in chapter two. Make your comments about the *behaviour* that has upset you, do not aim the criticism directly at the *person:*

'*Emma, when you leave your toys lying around the kitchen floor it makes me very cross because I keep falling over them and I might hurt myself.*'

Don't say:

'*Emma, you're such a naughty girl. I don't want to have to tell you again about leaving your toys lying around.*'

Try it now	1. Turn back to the list of feelings at the beginning of this chapter. Follow the above process with any of those feelings you found difficult to express or couldn't express effectively.
	2. Think of someone to whom you normally find it difficult to express your feelings. Bearing in mind what you have learned so far in this chapter, have a go at expressing your feelings to that person. For example, if you find it difficult to tell your best friend how happy you are that she has got a good job and is doing well at it, try telling her this in a way that will make her feel good.

Expressing feelings is a two-way process

So far in this chapter we have concentrated on helping *you* to express *your* feelings. Before moving on it is important to understand that expressing feelings should be a two-way process. Not only should you aim to help yourself in this respect, but if you are to gain maximum effect you should encourage other people to express their feelings too. If you are to build a better future, you need to know how other people feel about you and the things you do so that you can decide whether you need to make any changes. Remember it's up to you whether or not you want to – or feel you need to – change.

> Knowing how other people feel about you can give you a
> clearer picture on which to base your decision.

Creating the right environment

It also helps to know how people close to you feel about other
things in their life, otherwise you may harbour a false belief
about them. For example, you may not be aware that your
friend dislikes going to the supermarket with you on a Friday
evening to get the weekly food shopping unless she tells you.
On the face of it she may pretend to enjoy it because she
doesn't want to upset you but underneath she may think you're
a real pain-in-the-butt for dragging her along with you. She
may start making excuses not to go and then start avoiding you
in case you challenge her about it. Far better to prevent such a
situation arising by creating an environment in which people
are happy to say what they think without fear of upsetting
anyone – then she could have told you right at the start that
she didn't want to do it.

Feeling jealousy, envy and guilt

Earlier in this chapter we said that one of the consequences of
not being able to express your feelings can be that you often
feel jealous, envious or guilty. There is no place for any of these
emotions if you are to have a better life – you need to be able
to deal with them as soon as they arise – or better still, deal
with the underlying causes in order to *prevent* them arising in
the first place.

If you find you still suffer with any of these at the end of
this book then this is a clear sign that something is still out of
balance in your life. If this is the case we recommend that you
reread this book, ensuring that you are totally honest with
yourself. You are the only one being cheated if you hold back.

Dealing with jealousy, envy and guilt

Let's look at how you can help yourself to prevent or overcome
these emotions. If you have ever experienced feelings of
jealousy, envy or guilt, you will know how painful and

destructive they can be. It can also be difficult trying to get in touch with the real reason for this feeling. For example, on the surface it might appear that a woman is jealous of another woman her boyfriend is talking to because she thinks this other woman is prettier than her. But deep down inside the real reason for her jealousy might be that she is insecure because she doesn't know what her boyfriend thinks of her – because they never discuss their feelings!

And so she wastes energy being jealous, suspicious, mistrusting, etc. – she might even start to fantasise in her mind about what she thinks he is up to when she's not with him.

Discovering the cause

What can you do to stop this sort of thing happening to you? The simple answer is learn to talk openly about your feelings. By doing this you should be able to prevent the jealousy, envy or guilt arising – and as the old saying goes, *prevention is better than a cure*. However, if you are currently in a situation where you are suffering from any of these emotions let's look at how you can help yourself to find a cure.

The key is to try to get in touch with *why* you are feeling this emotion and then think of the most effective way you can handle it – a way that is going to resolve the situation, not start an argument or hurt the other person, because that is only going to make things worse! Also think about whether anything is out of balance in your life that might be making things worse. For example, are you spending too much money on socialising and holidays rather than saving up to buy the house of your dreams – and as a consequence suffering feelings of envy when you visit other people's beautiful houses?

To deal with this effectively will almost certainly involve talking to the other person about the events in the past that triggered the offending emotion. We'll look in more detail at how to do this later because although in theory it is simple, in practice it can be extremely difficult – especially if you are the sort of person who finds it difficult to talk about your feelings. Before we do this, let's spend a bit more time trying to understand the three emotions – jealousy, envy and guilt – because they can be enormously destructive if you do not or cannot deal with them.

Understanding jealousy, envy and guilt

If you look up the word *jealousy* in a dictionary you will find it explained as *possessiveness, insecurity, mistrust, apprehensive of being displaced in the love or goodwill of partner, lover, friend, etc.* The word *envy* is just as bad: *covetousness, ill-will, rivalry, begrudge, longing occasioned by another's good fortune.* Imagine the pain and waste of negative energy when envy pops up and says *I want that car* or *I should have won the lottery, not them.* Sadly, for people who suppress their feelings, this can happen all too often, and the jealousy or envy eats away at them. Once it gets into your system, it can become a way of life unless you take steps to deal with it.

What about guilt? The dictionary describes it using words like *remorse, shame, culpability.* Do you feel guilty about some of the things you have done, or not done, in your life? Guilt can be a very powerful emotion. It can lead a killer to confess to a crime he committed years ago because the pain caused by the guilt has become too much. Guilt can make people feel bad for refusing a friend who asked a favour – sometimes it can make them feel so bad that they end up saying yes even though they don't really want to.

Prevention is better than a cure

You might argue that it is right to feel jealous sometimes – for example if your partner frequently chats up someone else – or to feel guilty if you have done something wrong. We would counter that argument by saying that it's far better to prevent the feeling from arising in the first place by addressing the *cause* of it (remember the old adage – prevention is better than a cure). For example, if you know you shouldn't do something then *don't do it* – that way you won't create an environment in which you feel guilt. Or if your partner frequently chats up someone else, instead of feeling jealous find out why. Perhaps your own insecurity is a contributory factor? Talk to your partner about it and express how it makes you feel. If it continues to happen regularly and you really can't tolerate it, ask yourself why you are staying in a relationship where you are continually being hurt (is *because I love him* a good enough reason?).

> Jealousy, envy and guilt are all powerful emotions, and they tend to endure because of an inability to express feelings.

In order to deal with these emotions successfully it is first of all necessary to acknowledge them, to admit to yourself that you feel jealous, envious or guilty. If you cannot be honest with yourself you will find it difficult to deal with these three monsters!

Try it now In your notebook make three lists:

1. Who, or what, makes you jealous?

2. Who, or what, makes you envious? (If you have a problem distinguishing jealousy from envy, just do one list.)

3. Who, or what, makes you feel guilty?

Try to include everyone or everything that currently causes you to experience these emotions. Do not worry about saying why at this stage.

Taking the next step

Now that you have acknowledged what triggers these emotions, the next step is to deal with it. Only when you have done this can you take positive action to get rid of it or prevent it from happening again.

The following process can be extremely useful in helping you to deal with jealousy, envy or guilt:

Step 1. Acknowledge what you are *really* thinking, or why you *really* did what you did.

Step 2. Bombard it with logic until you can see how fruitless it is to feel this way.

Step 3. Think and act positively – do not give in to moaning or being negative. Admit to the feeling of jealousy, envy or guilt if it helps to get rid of it.

The following two examples will demonstrate how this works in practice.

Example 1

Imagine you are jealous or envious of a friend's new car.

Step 1. Acknowledge what you are really thinking, or why you really did what you did:

Logically you are thinking that it is a nice expensive car. If you didn't think this there would be no reason to be jealous or envious! So the first step in getting rid of the jealousy – and preventing it from happening in future – is to acknowledge your real feelings – the positive thoughts that the jealousy is masking. Accept that it's a nice, expensive car.

Step 2. Bombard it with logic until you can see how fruitless it is to feel this way:

Again applying logic, the next step is to ask yourself *What's wrong with my car?* Do I like it? Does it run okay? Why did I buy it in the first place? I chose it, so I must have liked it! It may not look much against your friend's brand new, gleaming motor, but how important is that in the grand scale of things? If you are envious because it's expensive and you couldn't afford it yourself, then what is the point in coveting it? Instead why not be pleased for your friend. Just as you would want him to be pleased for you if you had just bought the car!

Step 3. Think and act positively – do not give in to moaning or being negative. Admit to the feeling of jealousy, envy or guilt if it helps to get rid of it:

This is the real test of whether you can overcome your jealousy or not. If you adopt a *negative* attitude you will moan about your friend's car, lifestyle, etc. and you will generally look for anything negative, or spiteful, to say: 'Yeah, *it's not bad, but what made you choose red?*' (to your friend). '*What a waste of money*' (to other people). '*I'd rather have a BMW if I was going to spend that much on a car*' (to other people). '*It's only the bottom of the range model*' (to other people). Beware! The person with this sort of negative attitude is the sort of person who would like to go out and run a sharp object up the side of the nice new car because he is envious and knows that he can't afford one!

However, if you are to overcome this feeling of envy or jealousy, you will need to adopt a *positive* attitude. Acknowledge that you feel a touch of envy, but rather than keeping it inside and becoming bitter make sure you express your feelings to your friend (jokingly, if appropriate, but honestly). *'I love your new car – it looks great! I'm really quite envious.'* By getting the feelings out into the open there is little likelihood that they will build up inside, and possibly spoil the friendship. The envy may still be there in a mild form, but as a compliment not a resentment – it will inspire you, not make you bitter. If you really aspire to such a car yourself, you will do something *positive* about it – like work out how much it would cost, decide if you are prepared to make any sacrifices to have it, and start saving. Although when you look at it logically you may find that it is too expensive or it's not what you really want at all. It may just be a touch of wanting to keep up with the Joneses.

That's the crazy thing about jealousy and envy – often they're completely irrational.

> Status is buying something you don't want, with money you haven't got, to impress someone you don't like!

Example 2

Imagine you have refused to take your mother shopping on Saturday, but then feel terribly guilty about it.

Step 1. Acknowledge what you are really thinking, or why you really did what you did.

Having acknowledged that you are feeling guilty, the first step is to understand the *real* reason why you refused to go. Assume that it was because you wanted to give your house a good spring-clean. (This may or may not have been the reason you gave to your mother – you might have made an excuse because you thought the real reason wasn't good enough.)

Step 2. Bombard it with logic until you can see how fruitless it is to feel this way.

The second step is to apply logic. Ask yourself whether you think this is a good enough reason for saying no to your mother or are you just being selfish? You also need to consider whether your actions are simply wrong or harmful to your mother.

If your conscious is clear on both questions, then logically there is no reason to feel guilty – you must keep thinking this until you believe it. Until you believe it, you will either go on feeling guilty or letting your mother make you feel guilty.

If your conscience is *not* clear on one or both questions, you must decide what needs to be done to clear it. For example, if you have hurt or offended your mother badly perhaps you need to sit down and talk to her and explain clearly and honestly why you said no.

Step 3. Think and act positively – do not give in to moaning or being negative. Admit to the feeling of jealousy, envy or guilt if it helps to get rid of it.

If you adopt a *negative* attitude you will either say no and feel guilty, or say yes and end up doing something you don't want to.

However, if you have a *positive* attitude you will make sure that whenever you have to say no to someone you do it for a valid reason and do not make up excuses. You will deal with it in a positive way and will express how you are feeling, particularly if you still have twinges of guilt. Explain that you won't be able to go shopping with her this Saturday because you really need to clean your house. Say that you *can't help feeling a bit guilty* about not going with her but you want to get the house cleaned before your friend comes to stay next weekend. You don't always have to explain your reason, but it often helps soften the blow if you do. However, be careful – if you don't offer any explanation when saying no you can sometimes appear very cold and unhelpful. You must learn to accept that if the other person doesn't like you saying it that's their problem and not yours – they may be trying to make you feel guilty to get you to give in!

You may even find there is a compromise that can make

both parties happy – your mother might volunteer to come and help you clean the house so that you can still both go shopping together. But again beware! This is where you'll land yourself in trouble if you told a lie in the first place about why you didn't want to go shopping. It's best to be honest about it or you could still end up feeling guilty or doing something you don't want to.

Try it now	1. Refer to the lists you made earlier of the people or things that currently cause you to feel jealousy, envy or guilt. Follow the above three-step process to help you get to the root of these feelings and help you understand how you can overcome them if you want to. 2. Are you feeling brave? Deal with these emotions by talking to the person who is causing you to feel this way. To help you, remember everything you have learned in this chapter about expressing your feelings constructively and effectively. Remember too that until you deal with them they won't go away!

Summary

In this chapter you have looked at the advantages and disadvantages of expressing your feelings.

Advantages of expressing your feelings

◆ People know where they stand because they know how you feel about them or their words and actions.

◆ You can be yourself because you don't have to wear a mask to hide or disguise your feelings.

◆ You are far more influential because you don't carry any emotional baggage that can make you act irrationally.

◆ You rarely suffer from stress or depression because you don't internalise your feelings by keeping them to yourself.

◆ You find it much easier to talk about painful events from your past, like the death of a loved one, because you are in touch with your feelings.

◆ You are not embarrassed to cry if you are upset – whether it is at a funeral or a sad film.

Disadvantages of not expressing your feelings

- People don't know where they stand with you because they don't know what you are really thinking.

- People can get the impression that you are cold, hard or unfeeling, which can have an anti-influential effect.

- You often have to put on an act to disguise your true feelings, so the real you remains hidden from view. You may find yourself thinking that people don't understand you.

- You often suffer from stress, and possibly depression.

- You deny yourself the opportunity to benefit from other people's help or advice, because if you are unable to express how you feel they won't know if anything is wrong.

- You carry a lot of emotional baggage with you which can cloud your judgment and make you act irrationally in certain situations.

- As a consequence of not being able to express your feelings, you often feel jealous, envious or guilty.

You learned a process to help you overcome any difficulty you might have in expressing your feelings:

Step 1

Discover the source of your discomfort.

Step 2

List the disadvantages and possible consequences of not expressing this feeling.

Step 3

List the advantages and likely outcomes of expressing this feeling.

And finally you discovered that a potential consequence of not being able to express your feelings is that you suffer from jealousy, envy or guilt. In order to deal with these destructive emotions you were introduced to another process:

Step 1

Acknowledge what you are *really* thinking, or why you *really* did what you did.

Step 2

Bombard it with logic until you can see how fruitless it is to feel this way.

Step 3

Think and act positively – do not give in to moaning or being negative. Admit to the feeling of jealousy, envy or guilt if it helps to get rid of it.

*No-one can
make you feel
inferior without
your consent.*
ELEANOR
ROOSEVELT

CHAPTER 7

Becoming More Assertive

H ave you ever found yourself using phrases like:

- 'Well, okay I don't mind helping you' when you actually *do* mind because you had other plans.
- 'I don't want to be a nuisance but...'
- 'I'm really sorry to bother you...'
- 'It was fine, I'm just not very hungry' to the waiter who asks if your meal was okay, but you don't want to cause a fuss by saying it wasn't.

Or do you sometimes find yourself making excuses or telling lies because you think it sounds better to make an excuse than to say you don't want to do something?

- 'I'm sorry I won't be able to come to your party – my sister and her family are coming to visit me.'
- 'Oh what a shame you didn't ask me to baby-sit sooner – I've arranged to go out that night.'
- 'I'd like to help you but I've got to go to a meeting this afternoon.'
- 'I'm afraid I won't be able to meet you on Wednesday after all – something else has just come up and I can't get out of it.'

> Lacking natural assertiveness is a common failing which can result in others taking advantage of you.

You will try to avoid potential conflict or be reluctant to put across any point you feel strongly about because you either get upset about it or are worried about upsetting someone else.

Non-assertive people often experience anxiety, tension and even physical aches and pains in any situation that involves openly disagreeing with others. They avoid doing or saying anything they think will upset someone else, often at their own inconvenience. Take the following example of the former, non-assertive, Frank Gilbert:

Case Study

'Years ago I used to lack confidence in my own ability. Although outwardly I appeared very confident – talking loudly, arguing for the sake of it – I had no real belief in the points I was making. People believed the act I was putting on, but inside me was a total lack of confidence, a lot of pain, confusion and turmoil.

I had a reputation for being a good sport which made me feel good but often cost me dear! If I was embarking on a journey from London to Bristol and a friend asked for a lift to Birmingham – vaguely in the same direction, but miles out of my way – I would take him! I was desperate to be liked and loved. Because of this I could never say no to other people's often unreasonable requests. I would lend money to so-called friends, knowing that I was unlikely to ever get it back. I couldn't really afford to lend this money, but I needed their love and approval so I lent it to them rather than upset them by saying no.

I would go along with the crowd, very rarely doing what I wanted to do, going along with others wishes just to keep the peace. I was an easy touch for my friends. All of this caused me an enormous amount of self-loathing and frustration. At times my frustration would turn to aggression – I would flip my lid!

I relied on others to chat up the girls and make the first move, often ending up with the girl that no-one else wanted. It was painful for me to walk into a party or a pub where I knew I would encounter strangers.

Nearly everything I did was for other people, because I needed their approval and their love. I lived my life trying to be perfect, not taking risks in case I made a mistake and upset someone. I had far too high expectations of others, and so time and time again others let me down.

I had big hang-ups about people in authority, believing they had to be right all of the time and consequently never putting forward my point of view if it contradicted theirs. I became nervous and often talked gibberish in the company of an authoritative figure, particularly if I was asked to express my opinion. If it was different to theirs I quickly changed it, saying that I hadn't thought it through yet.

I hero-worshipped people who impressed me with their apparent assertiveness. At the same time I carried a lot of guilt for not being able to get across a point that I believed in, or for doing things I didn't want to do. I had knots in my stomach when I had to do something new or meet new people. On the rare occasions that I made decisions I often made the wrong ones – or so I believed.

I put other people in my life in front of me, believing that they were more important than I was. I certainly didn't value myself. If someone did something for me I would go over-the-top thanking them, until in the end they got sick of my gratitude. I would be embarrassed if anyone paid me a compliment, shrugging it off or passing the credit on to someone else.

I had tremendous problems asking for a favour or for help. When I plucked up the courage to ask I was always very humble and apologetic: 'I'm sorry to ask...', 'If you wouldn't mind...', 'I'll pay you back tenfold...'

I worried constantly about what people thought of me, always becoming defensive or blaming others if I was criticised. I thought criticism meant that someone didn't like me, or they were angry with me. I rarely admitted making a mistake, instead I internalised the pain. This lowered my self-esteem even further until I felt pretty worthless and unlovable.' _____

> You can overcome a lack of assertiveness. By becoming more assertive you can become happier. People do not respect a lack of assertiveness – but they *do* take advantage of it!

What makes people unassertive?

In one word, *conditioning*! Remember the parents, teachers or other adults who said that little children should be seen and not heard? That they should be quiet – only speak when they are spoken to? Consequently many children become submissive or will only say something when asked, for fear of upsetting someone else. Others will rebel and become aggressive because they think that is the only way to be heard – they've seen it work for the grown-ups so it must be okay.

Conditioning can also play a part in making you unassertive as you grow up. If you were constantly ignored or talked over, told off or laughed at for getting things wrong or put down for expressing your opinion, this could have contributed towards making you feel that you are not important. This can lead to low self-esteem which can result in you being unassertive because you don't believe you have anything worthwhile to say – it's a real downhill spiral.

> People who are unassertive do not value themselves enough, or love themselves.

One of the major causes of unassertive behaviour is fear of self-expression. This fear is often based on unreasonable, but commonly-held, beliefs:

'I have to be approved of, or loved, for everything that I do'

This fear often originates from childhood, from being criticised for being naughty, bad or useless. Yet this fear need never have arisen if the criticism had been aimed at the child's *behaviour* rather than the child itself. Remember what you learned in chapter two about this. It is far less harmful to say '*it's naughty to throw stones at your sister*' than it is to say '*you're a very naughty boy*'.

For many children such all-encompassing criticism can lead them to believe that their parents will not love them if they are naughty. Consequently in adult life this can lead to a fear of speaking out, of doing something differently, in case it leads to disapproval or makes them unlovable. Hence they become quiet, unassuming and unassertive so as not to risk losing someone else's love or approval.

But let's look at this logically. How can anyone expect to please all of the people all of the time? If this is the case, why get hung up on trying? If you lost someone's friendship because you were assertive, what sort of a friend was that person anyway?

Think about what was said in chapter five about loving yourself. If you don't love yourself, how can you expect other people to love you?

> One sure way to not love yourself is to go through life being unassertive and letting other people walk all over you.

People are unlikely to respect you if you don't show that you respect yourself. Only if you respect yourself can you hope to love yourself. And once you love yourself, you won't worry if you have to speak your mind or say no to someone because you will no longer fear earning their disapproval or losing their love or respect. You will recognise how irrational it is to think that way and thus you will find it easier to remove it from your way of thinking.

'I must be perfect in all that I undertake'

Many people, as they progress through life, set unrealistically high standards for themselves and their own performance. Consequently they often find themselves disappointed and see themselves as failures when they fail to meet these self-imposed unrealistic standards. This in turn can lead into the downward spiral of not valuing themselves, having low self-esteem, feeling worthless etc.

Once again our old friend conditioning has a lot to answer for here! Many parents have unrealistic expectations of their children's abilities. Many expect their children to pass all their exams at school and some even offer them 'bribes' to do it – a new bicycle, a new pair of trainers, a trip to the adventure playground... This can lead the child to fear losing his parents approval or love – as well as missing out on the reward from the bribe – if he is anything less than perfect.

There is often an implied expectation that the child should be perfect, even though the parents were often far from perfect themselves when they were at school. Many parents project their *own* hopes and ambitions onto their children, wanting them to have the life – qualifications, job, status, etc – that they themselves would have liked but often failed to achieve.

At work unrealistic demands are often made on the employee, so much so that millions of working days are lost each year through stress or stress-related illnesses.

One of the unfortunate consequences of all these demands and expectations, from parents, teachers and employers, can be that some people are afraid to try anything new or different for fear of failing or being seen as inadequate. By striving for perfection and failing to take risks or explore unfamiliar situations, many people are unable to let their real self show through – they are constantly wearing a mask that conceals who they are, and that can cause them a great deal of turmoil inside.

But nobody is perfect! How do you define *perfect* anyway? Surely it is subjective? Could humankind ever agree on *one* definition of a perfect person? It's doubtful, so why strive to be something that can't even be defined – that's a recipe for frustration and failure!

By all means strive to do things well, but do not berate yourself if you feel you have been less than perfect.

'My happiness is in the hands of others'

This is another common misconception amongst unassertive people, believing that their happiness is in the hands of others rather than in their own hands. This leads them to seek the approval of others for almost everything they do, and often means doing things they don't want to because that is the only way to win approval. They become submissive, believing that they can only be happy if they make everyone else happy first.

You have already seen that it is illogical to expect to be able to make everyone happy all of the time. Why then do so many people act as if this is the only way to progress through life? Do they really believe that their own happiness lies in making everyone else happy? Can they only be happy if they have everyone else's approval?

Perhaps the greatest danger in acting as if your happiness lies in the hands of others is that you will always suppress your own needs in favour of others and thus, ironically, never experience the true happiness that can only come through valuing and loving yourself.

Defining assertiveness

Many people confuse assertiveness with aggression, thinking that if someone is loud or behaves in an aggressive way he or she is an assertive person. Wrong!

One of the best explanations of assertiveness we have come across can be found in an excellent book called *Putting Assertiveness to Work* by Graham Willcocks and Steve Morris. They suggest that being assertive means taking into account other people's feelings whilst having the right to put across your own point of view in a constructive and non-threatening way. Each part of this definition is important in its own right and is worth further explanation.

'Taking into account other people's feelings'

By thinking about how the other person will feel *before* you say anything, it gives you the opportunity to think about how best to put your message across. How would *you* feel if you were on the receiving end? A little forethought can often prevent an upset or misunderstanding.

Taking into account other people's feelings also means accepting that sometimes you *are* going to upset the other person. You need to rationalise this. Often this happens because they have done something to warrant it, (like taking advantage of you, or doing something they know they shouldn't do,) or because by not being assertive you will end up saying yes when actually you want to say no.

'Having the right to put across your own point of view'

If you don't believe that you have the right to put across your own point of view you will struggle to be assertive. Think about it logically for a moment. Your point of view is every bit as important, and has every bit as much right to be heard, as anyone else's. It doesn't mean that it's right, or that other people have to agree with it, but it *is* your point of view and it is your right to put it across. Don't be put off by the fact that other people may challenge it or disagree with it – that's their right!

If you fear being challenged about it, think carefully about your reasons for holding that point of view. Are they good, solid reasons? Are they your own reasons, or do you hold that point of view because of your conditioning? For example, are you anti-smoking because *you* believe smoking is harmful to your health, or is it because your parents are anti-smoking and that's how you've been brought up. But if challenged could you really say why?

> One of the greatest barriers to being assertive is not having a strong enough reasons to support the point you want to make.

Not being able to support your point of view can result in aggression if you are not careful – or it might result in you withholding your point of view. Imagine that you have to tell one of the girls who works for you that her skirt is too short. The first point you need to be very clear about is exactly who is saying so? Do *you* think her skirt is too short? Is it *your boss* who thinks her skirt is too short, or does *company policy* say that her skirt is too short? This will affect the way you speak to her about it.

Let's assume it's *your* point of view. Ask yourself why you hold that point of view – what are your reasons for telling her that her skirt is too short? Are they good, solid reasons – in which case tell her honestly, or are they caused by jealousy – perhaps the boss pays more attention to her than to you. Or don't you really know why? If they are anything other than good, solid reasons then you may struggle to put your point across assertively.

'Expressing your point of view in a constructive and non-threatening way'

This is another vital part of the equation, and is one of the fundamental differences between being assertive and being aggressive.

> An assertive person will always put their point across in a constructive and non-threatening way, whereas an aggressive person will tend to shout and make threats.

Shouting and making threats rarely achieves respect! It may achieve immediate results, but if there is no respect then the long term consequences may outweigh the short term gain.

It can take forethought and planning to get this bit right. Not everyone is capable of doing this spontaneously, although the more you practice the easier it becomes. It is worth taking the time to think about what you want to say and how you are going to say it to gain maximum effect. Listen to what other people say when they are trying to put across a point and learn from their mistakes as well as their good points.

The benefits of being assertive

A good way to think of assertive behaviour is as the opposite of inhibited behaviour. Being assertive is about creating a *win-win* situation, where everyone knows where they stand. It is about being polite, but firm. It has the added benefit of being able to help you feel good about yourself after you have dealt with a difficult situation or person.

For some people it can be difficult and uncomfortable to be assertive, but it is one of those situations where, once you have mastered it, the gain from getting there far outweighs the pain of the journey.

Being assertive is a vital component in helping you to have a better life. As you have already learned, if you are not assertive you are very likely to end up living out someone else's life script rather than your own.

Understanding how negative beliefs are destructive

Sadly for many people living an assertive lifestyle is just a dream, and will remain that way. Their conditioning makes the prospect of becoming assertive seem unreal, they do not believe that it can apply to them because they think they were not born to be assertive. Belief is one of the most powerful tools available to humankind. Unfortunately many people choose to make *negative* beliefs their master. They talk themselves into believing that they are not meant to have what they want out of life, that other people are somehow *luckier* or *more successful* than them.

Negative beliefs are dangerous things in that they can become self-fulfilling prophecies.

Case study

'Years ago, when I was disillusioned with my job as a training manager, I applied for the role of Head of Training with a newly formed life assurance company in the north of England. I knew that I had all the qualifications to do the job and I knew that I would make an enormous success of it, because I had been doing a very similar job successfully for the past three years.

I was thrilled when I got invited to an interview.

However, by the time I actually went for the interview I had started to have doubts about whether I was suitable for the job or not. I started thinking what would happen if I made a mess of it because I'd never had to manage that many people before. In addition I wasn't sure if I wanted to move house again. I worried about losing the job and not being able to afford the mortgage.

Needless to say, at the interview all of these doubts found their way to the forefront of my mind. The interviewer asked me some probing questions – all of which I had anticipated because of my own experience at recruitment – and instead of being positive and enthusiastic I gave her some vague and unconvincing answers.

I didn't get the job. But I learned a very valuable lesson – that my words and actions reflect my beliefs, and if those beliefs are negative then the outcome is likely to be negative too.

I have never made that mistake again. If I know that I can do something, and I know that I want to do it, then everything about me is positive – my attitude, my beliefs, my words, my body language, my enthusiasm. All of it. Because if I don't believe in what I want, why should I think I am entitled to have it?' _____

Being positive

Ironically in situations like the one above, you will find that you get what you *believe*, not necessarily what you *want*! The good news is that *positive* beliefs can become self-fulfilling prophecies too!

> If you believe that you are going to succeed at something – truly believe it, not just pretend that you believe it, or put on a mask of belief – then you stand a far greater chance of success.

Walt Disney, Richard Branson, Anita Roddick are examples of visionaries, positive thinkers and believers in themselves and their ability to succeed.

A characteristic that is possessed by many people who have achieved their goals – not just famous people, but ordinary people too – is assertiveness. Assertiveness manifests itself in a number of ways: through words, body language, actions, attitudes, beliefs. Below we have focused on some of the most common attributes that assertive people possess:

They believe that their views are as valuable as anyone else's.

They will not be intimidated when discussing matters close to their heart and will speak their mind without fear or favour. Their views will be well thought out and convincingly communicated.

They believe that everyone has certain rights:
- To have, and express, their own opinions and beliefs.
- To have, and put forward, ideas.
- To be heard and listened to.
- To have feelings.
- To be treated fairly.
- To say they don't understand or they don't know.
- To disagree with someone else's opinion or belief.
- To be forgiven if they make a mistake or say something wrong.

Equally they believe that everyone has a responsibility:
- To acknowledge that other people also have those rights.
- To share their ideas and opinions with others rather than keep them to themselves.
- To behave in a constructive and adult manner rather than be petulant or aggressive.

They talk about their talents and successes openly and without embarrassment.

They will be proud of their achievements, but never boastful! They will give credit to others where credit is due, but will not shy away from acknowledging their own contribution to their success.

They accept and knowledge a deserved compliment.

They will say thank you when paid a compliment. They will not dismiss it by saying that anyone could have done it or it wasn't difficult.

They accept criticism without becoming defensive.

Accepting criticism can be a problem for many people – they take it as a personal attack rather than a comment about their behaviour, appearance or something similar. Often this is a result of the way the criticism is made: *'You're hopeless at writing letters'* rather than *'There are some spelling mistakes in your letter – would you like to me point them out to you?'*

Unassertive people often react to criticism by becoming defensive or blaming other people. Assertive people take the criticism on board, weigh it up and respond appropriately.

They might simply thank you or ask why you said what you did. They will rarely be hurt by the criticism but will question it or comment on it if they feel it is not constructive. They will want to learn from it.

They admit that they have made a mistake.

Everyone makes mistakes! Assertive people will say sorry if it's appropriate rather than trying to deny that it was their fault. Most importantly, they will learn from their mistakes so as not to repeat them. They will find a different and better, or more appropriate way to do it next time.

They ask a favour without being apologetic.

They will not be afraid or feel the need to apologise for asking someone to do something for them. They will not feel the need to preface the request with 'I'm sorry to bother you but...' Neither will they shy away from asking for the return of a borrowed item. 'Could you let me have that book back that I lent you two months ago please?' instead of 'I'm sorry to be a pain, but I could really do with having that book back that I lent you a couple of months ago if you've finished with it!'

Look at it this way. If you feel you have to apologise for asking the favour, why are you asking it in the first place? You're not really *sorry*, you're probably just a bit embarrassed because you don't want to upset or offend the person because that might make them angry with you or make them dislike you. If your request is a reasonable one then you shouldn't feel any need to apologise for making it. If it's unreasonable, that's a different matter – perhaps you shouldn't be making it?

They complain when it's justified.

How many times have you received poor goods or service and put up with it because you didn't want to – or weren't sure how to – complain to the provider? Perhaps you have had a bad meal at a restaurant some time but, instead of sending the food back, you have moaned to your family and friends about it afterwards.

Assertive people will say if goods or services do not meet their expectations. This has two main benefits. It gives the *provider* the opportunity to put it right, and learn from his mistake, and it also gives *you* the chance to obtain the goods or service you were expecting.

They comment about being interrupted by others.

Do you ever find yourself being interrupted, or talked over, and you don't say a word about it? Do you suffer in silence? Do you sulk? Do you interrupt back, or do you moan to someone else about it?

People who interrupt other people need to know that their interruption is anti-influential, otherwise they will continue to do it. Often it has become so habitual that they don't even realise they are doing it. Many good ideas must have gone unheard over the years through interruptions!

Assertive people will not suffer in silence if they are interrupted. They will politely, but firmly, let the other person know how they feel by saying 'Excuse me, you have just interrupted me – I haven't finished what I was saying.'

Becoming more assertive

We have already established that assertiveness is one of the areas that many people struggle with and as a consequence of not being assertive they can suffer unnecessarily, both personally and professionally. We have also cautioned you about confusing being assertive with being aggressive. This can be a barrier to becoming more assertive because if you believe that you have to be aggressive in order to be assertive you may not find the idea appealing.

> Remember, being assertive is about reaching a win-win situation when dealing with other people.

Reaching a win-win situation may result in having to compromise on one or both parts, but the important point is that no one should end up feeling that they have lost.

The following simple process can help you to put your point across in an assertive way. If you learn the process and practice it regularly you will soon find that it becomes second nature. Don't worry if it feels strange at first – it's bound to if you're not used to being assertive, and yet once you become familiar with it it seems so obvious and so logical you'll wonder why you didn't use it before.

Step 1. State your own feelings or point of view or expectations in a clear, polite and constructive manner. Never use apologetic or sarcastic language and do not waffle.

Step 2. Listen to what the other person has to say and acknowledge his feelings or point of view or response.

Step 3. Agree a mutually convenient way forward.

It's worth issuing a warning before we look at how this works in practice. Each of these three steps is equally important – if you miss one out you risk appearing submissive, or aggressive, or judgmental. The first two steps may be repeated if necessary and may also be reversed – it will depend on whether you are initiating the discussion or responding to someone else's comments.

Let's look at some examples of how it works. In practice each example could take several different turns. However, for the purpose of demonstrating the process we will just look at one potential way of dealing with it.

Example 1

You are with your partner having a meal in a restaurant. The steaks that you have ordered are tough. You decide to send them back and order something different and you call the waiter over.

Step 1

State your own feelings or point of view or expectations in a clear, polite and constructive manner. Never use apologetic or sarcastic language and do not waffle
Be polite but firm '*Excuse me, these steaks are tough. We'd like to change them for something else please.*'

Much of the impact would be lost if you just said '*Excuse me, these steaks are tough.*' To make full and effective use of the process, being assertive requires you to state what you want to happen about the tough steaks '*We'd like to change them for something else please.*'

Do not begin by apologising to the waiter '*I'm sorry to trouble you...*' – that it *not* being assertive, it is being submissive!

Step 2

Listen to what the other person has to say and acknowledge his feelings/point of view/response

The most likely response is that the waiter will apologise and offer to replace the steaks.

Remember to acknowledge his response: '*Thank you.*' In this instance you may need to repeat your original request too, otherwise you may end up with two more steaks! '*We'd like to order something different please. May we see the menu?*'

Let's now assume that the waiter is reluctant to let you *change* your order, although he would be happy to *replace* the steaks.

You will need to return to stating your own feelings or point of view or expectations. '*I'm disappointed at your reluctance. The steaks are tough and we'd like to change them for something else please.*'

Whatever you do, resist the temptation to back down or make threats – '*If you don't change them we'll leave the restaurant without paying the bill*', or be sarcastic to the waiter. It might not be his fault.

Remain calm but firm.

Step 3

Agree a mutually convenient way forward

Remember the aim here is to get a win-win situation, not for one party to end up feeling superior to the other – assertiveness is not about being superior. It is important, whenever possible, that everyone is happy with the way forward, even if it means accepting a compromise. Compromising, in this context, does not mean giving in – it means weighing up the options and arriving at a mutually convenient way forward. The way forward might just be a sensible next step – it will not necessarily be the final solution.

In this example let's assume you agree that the waiter will

bring you a menu to look at while he checks with his boss if it is okay to change your order. This is a reasonable compromise *at this stage*. The waiter knows you're not happy about the steaks and that he has got to check whether you can change your order, whilst you understand that it's not his fault and ask to look at a menu whilst he sorts it out.

It is important to remain assertive whatever the outcome. If necessary ask to speak to the manager. If you are not happy with what he says, tell him so – follow all three steps with the manger. Only as a last resort should you leave the restaurant without having had the meal you want or without paying. Even then, do it assertively, not in a fit of temper.

Example 2

A colleague at work asks you to lend him £20 until pay day in two weeks time. He often ask you to lend him money and you have always obliged in the past even though this has sometimes left you short yourself. He has always paid you back, although often he has borrowed the money again a couple of days later.

You cannot afford to lend him the £20 he is asking for, neither do you want to lend him any more money in the future. So, when he asks you to lend him £20:

Step 1

State your own feelings or point of view or expectations in a clear ear, polite and constructive manner. Never use apologetic or sarcastic language and do not waffle
Tell him politely, *'I can't afford to lend you £20, I need it myself. It puts me in an awkward position when you keep asking me to lend you money because I feel bad if I refuse you, but then I leave myself short. I would appreciate it if you didn't ask me again, then I wouldn't end up feeling bad about having to say no.'*

Remember to be *clear, polite and constructive* – whatever you do don't start waffling, making excuses or apologising for not wanting to lend him *your* money!

Step 2

Listen to what the other person has to say and acknowledge

his or her feelings/point of view/response

There's a fair chance your response will take him by surprise and might even embarrass him. He may try to talk you into lending it to him just this once.

Let's imagine he says *'I won't ask again, but I'm really stuck. I'd be ever so grateful if you would help me out – even if it's only £10?'*

Acknowledge his response, but don't give in to him. Say that you're sorry he's in this position, but you really can't help him. Remind him you need the money yourself.

Step 3

Agree a mutually convenient way forward

Try to help him find a solution rather than just leaving it there. Look for a solution that will stop him from having to ask you or anyone else in the future if he can borrow money. Ask him if he'd thought about looking at what he earns and what he spends to see why he keeps running short. Offer to help him go over his finances – but only if you *want* to, not just because you feel you *ought* to!

It is important in situations like this that you do not end up feeling guilty. If you find this happening, go back over the situation and look at it logically and dispassionately. Firstly, *he* got himself into this situation – it was not your fault that he overspent. Secondly, *you* need the money yourself. Thirdly, if you go on lending him money whenever he asks he will go on taking advantage of your generosity and will not learn to take responsibility for sorting out his finances. This could land him in much greater trouble later. Finally, if he breaks off the friendship because you wouldn't lend him the money you would have to question what sort of a friend he was in the first place. He was probably just using you.

Try it now

Think of an issue that you need to deal with assertively or one that you should have dealt with assertively in the recent past but didn't. Following the above process, think carefully about what you want to say and plan how you are going to say it. Think about the words you want to use and the points you want to make. Write it down if it helps. Rehearse it – say it out loud or ask someone you trust if you can practice it on them.

If appropriate, go out and do it for real. But please remember to listen to the response you get and react accordingly otherwise it will sound like you're reading from as script and you're going to stick to it at all costs – like a bad sales person!

When you have done this, go over it again in your mind. Did it go well? If not, why not? What could you have done differently? Did you miss out any of the steps in the process?

Making a proposal

We are going to look at something else that can help you become more assertive, particularly if you sometimes find it difficult to put your ideas across, or put forward suggestions. Perhaps you have been ignored, or laughed at, or shot down in flames in the past when you have tried? Maybe the thought of having to put across a difficult or unpopular suggestion makes you nervous?

There are times when you may find it very useful to put forward your ideas in the form of a *proposal*. This has several benefits:

◆ It is brief and to the point, therefore it saves time.
◆ By making specific points you avoid waffling or prolonged explanations.
◆ You can target the benefits at the listener's needs, thus making it more likely that your proposal will be accepted.
◆ In many cases you can plan what you want to say beforehand and rehearse it.

> Making a proposal can be very effective at achieving results, or moving a discussion forward.

The following, simple to learn, process can help you to make assertive proposals. It consists of three parts:

Step 1. Let the other person know you are about to make a proposal which you will support with some reasons – *'I have a proposal to make, followed by...reasons'*.

Step 2. State your proposal *'My proposal is...'*.

Step 3. State your reasons – *'My first reason is... My second reason is...'*.

Let's examine this in a bit more detail, then we'll show you some examples of how to follow the process.

Step 1. Let the other person know you are about to make a proposal which you will support with some reasons – 'I have a proposal to make, followed by... reasons'.

By telling the other person you are going to make a proposal supported by some reasons, you are giving notice of your intentions and at the same time gaining their attention. The impact may be partly lost if you do not flag this up at the outset.

Always try to support your proposal with two to three strong reasons. The power of the proposal lies in the strength of the reasons.

Step 2. State your proposal 'My proposal is...'.

Use positive, clear and concise language to make your proposal if you want to gain maximum effect. Always begin by saying 'My proposal is...'.

Do not say things like *'I think* we should...' or *'I'd* like to...' This can weaken the proposal and make it sound as though it is for your own benefit rather than the person's to whom you are talking.

Step 3. State your reasons 'My first reason is... My second reason is...'.

Always remember to follow up your proposal with reasons, otherwise it may have very little impact. If people don't know your reasons they won't necessarily understand why you are making the proposal.

◆ It is very important not to let anyone interrupt you before you start to give your reasons, or, indeed, before you have finished.

◆ Think very carefully about the number of reasons you need to give – this can be the make or break of the proposal.

◆ *One* reason may not have sufficient impact unless it is a very strong one.

◆ *Two* reasons are ideal, provided they are both good ones.

♦ *Three* reasons may be appropriate in certain circumstances if they all add strength to the proposal.

♦ *Four* or more reasons are normally too many – the impact will be lost.

♦ The most important point to remember when giving your reasons is that they need to appeal to your listener(s). When you are preparing your reasons, ask yourself what you would be looking for if you were on the receiving end. You risk getting your proposal rejected if the reasons you give are for your own benefit rather than your listener's.

Example 1

Your partner smokes about 20 cigarettes a day. You are a non-smoker. You want to propose that he gives up smoking.

The wrong way to say it is:

'I think you should give up smoking. It's a disgusting habit and I hate the smell – it gets on my clothes and in my hair.'

This is the wrong way to say it for two reasons. Firstly, it does not flag the fact that you are going to make a proposal followed by two reasons. The impact it makes is more like a reprimand or a bolt out of the blue. Secondly, there is no benefit in it for the listener, the reasons given are for the benefit of the speaker only.

Another, more effective way of making your proposal would be:

'I've got a proposal, which I'm making for two reasons. My proposal is that you give up smoking (do not let the listener interrupt you at this stage!). My first reason is that you would save about £20 a week which would go a long way towards paying for our holiday in the Caribbean. My second reason is that you should get rid of that awful cough you've got which you said makes you feel sick.'

Can you see the difference? You may still not persuade your partner to give up smoking, but you stand a far better chance if you try this way. The reasons given are for your partner's benefit, not just yours. This not only makes the proposal sound more attractive, but it also takes away any elements of 'selfishness'.

Example 2

You are in a meeting at work that is going on and on without achieving anything. You want a break and you also want to move the meeting forward. The wrong way to suggest this would be:

'I'm getting really fed up with this, we're not getting anywhere. I'm going for a break!'

A more effective way would be:

'I've got a proposal to make followed by two reasons. My proposal is that we take a fifteen minute break. My first reason is that we've been here for two hours and I'm sure we could all do with a break and a cup of coffee. My second reason is that it will give us all a chance to reflect on what's been happening and get our thoughts together so that when we come back in we can move the meeting forward.'

Try it now

Think of a time when you could have followed the above process to make a proposal, but didn't. Following the above process, think carefully about what you wanted to say and plan how you could have said it. Write it down if it helps. Rehearse it – say it out loud or ask someone you trust if you can practice it on them.

Next time you come across a situation where you feel you could achieve a good result by following this process, go out and do it for real.

When you have done this, go over it again in your mind: Did it go well? If not, why not? What could you have done differently? Did you miss out any of the steps in the process?

Persevering to get it right

In striving to become more assertive you will probably gain the most benefit from trying it out in low risk situations first. Get the feel of it. Learn to enjoy it. Let it become a natural way of life, then move on to more complex situations – ones that you would normally avoid at all costs but which have left you feeling frustrated because you *have* avoided them!

Even if you don't always get the result you wanted, don't

give up. Analyse what went wrong and resolve to learn from it so that you don't make the same mistake again. If the other person got aggressive or pulled rank, could you have done anything to prevent it? It may even be that nothing went wrong – sometimes the person you come up against is just simply more assertive than you are! Learn from this too – what did he or she do that made them more assertive? Is it something that you could do too?

Summary

In this chapter you looked at how conditioning plays a large part in making people assertive or unassertive. In order to become more assertive you need to get rid of beliefs such as:

- ◆ 'I have to be approved of or loved for everything that I do.'
- ◆ 'I must be perfect in all that I undertake.'
- ◆ 'My happiness is in the hands of others.'

You also learned that assertive people:

- ◆ Believe that their views are as valuable as anyone else's.
- ◆ Believe that everyone has certain rights and responsibilities.
- ◆ Talk about their talents and successes openly and without embarrassment.
- ◆ Accept and acknowledge a deserved compliment.
- ◆ Accept criticism without becoming defensive.
- ◆ Admit that they have made a mistake.
- ◆ Ask a favour without being apologetic.
- ◆ Complain when it's justified.
- ◆ Comment about being interrupted by others.

To help you become more assertive we introduced you to a simple process:

Step 1

State your own feelings or point of view or expectations in a clear, polite and constructive manner. Never use apologetic or sarcastic language and do not waffle.

Step 2

> Listen to what the other person has to say and acknowledge his feelings or point of view or response.

Step 3

> Agree a mutually convenient way forward.

We also showed you how to make a proposal effectively in order to put across your ideas:

Step 1

> Let the other person know you are about to make a proposal which you will support with some reasons.

Step 2

> State your proposal.

Step 3

> State your reasons.

CHAPTER 8

Overcoming Fear

F ear is a strange thing – it can affect people in so many different ways. It is something that touches everyone's life at some stage, to a greater or lesser degree and yet rather than acknowledging this and learning how to deal with it, many people let it rule their lives. Phobias are fears taken to the extreme and for those who suffer from them they know how life-destroying they can be.

On the plus side, fear is a natural part of survival, and as such can be a positive thing. The human brain and nervous system are programmed to react automatically to numerous problems and challenges in the environment. For example, if you are confronted with a charging bull in a field you do not need to stop and think about what to do – fear pumps the adrenaline and tells you to *run*! Fear therefore has a necessary part to play in our survival.

However, it is when fear gets in your way and prevents personal growth that something needs to be done about it. In this chapter you will be confronting your fears and learning to deal with them. Learning to deal with fear in an appropriate way is another very important part of building a new future and is the last big hurdle that you need to clear in this book before you can move forward.

We said a minute ago that fear can prevent personal growth, and it is this type of fear as opposed to phobias that we will be dealing with in this chapter. The processes you will be introduced to *can* also be used to help overcome phobias, however many people require professional help in this respect as they are unable to deal with the phobia on their own.

Case Study _____

'When I was 29 my mother died of breast cancer. She was just 58 years old, one of the kindest, gentlest people I have ever known. From the moment the tumour was diagnosed as malignant she was, not unnaturally, terrified that she was going to die – as indeed she did ten months later. To this day I firmly believe that her fear contributed to her death. However, this cannot be scientifically proven, nor is it the main point that I want to make.

The point I want to make is about how my own fears came into play in this situation and how they prevented me from fully appreciating those last ten months of my mother's life. Let me list my fears:

◆ I was afraid to talk to her about the past in case she thought I was writing her off, consequently there are many things about her that I will never know and, about my own childhood.

◆ I was afraid to talk about the future because I knew she didn't believe she had one and I didn't want to upset her by talking about things she didn't think she'd live to see.

◆ I was afraid to speak to the doctors in depth to ask about her cancer because I was afraid of what they'd say, so I never really understood very much about it – I certainly never expected her to die and it was a huge shock when she did.

◆ I was afraid to question more than once the opinion of the doctor who assured me that my mother's agonising headaches were a normal reaction to the chemotherapy. So I carried on giving her the pain-killers that he prescribed, which still left her in dreadful pain. Imagine my horror when her regular doctor returned from his holidays a few days later and rushed her straight into hospital. She died shortly afterwards.

◆ I was afraid to talk to my brothers and my husband about it – because I didn't want to upset them any more than I had to – and I was afraid I'd break down in tears. Hence I bottled it all up inside.

◆ I was afraid to take too much time off work in case I let people down – I was involved in a very important project at the time. Consequently I was not there when my mother died and I was left with an enormous feeling of guilt and selfishness because I thought I should have done more for her.

After she died I lived for years with the dreadful guilt that I had let her down and felt that somehow if I'd acted differently she might have been alive today.

Preventing personal growth

How can fear prevent personal growth? Well, for a start it can stop you from realising your full potential by making you a prisoner of your own insecurities. It can prevent you from taking the risks that are necessary for personal growth and success because it undermines your confidence. In this context fear is linked very closely to low self-esteem and lack of self-belief because when you stop growing as a person your self-esteem will diminish and the resulting lack of confidence can affect every part of your life. For example, if you have been turned down for a job in the past you may be afraid to apply for another job in case you get rejected again. At the same time you suffer from low self-esteem which results from being turned down and from your belief that you wouldn't get the job anyway because you were not good enough. This is a recipe for failure. What you need to do is learn how to turn it into a recipe for success.

Identifying what you fear

Let's begin by identifying the things that *you* fear, however large or small, and look at how this fear can hold you back.

> One of the great disadvantages of fearing something is that it can actually prevent you in some way from leading the life that you want because of the adverse reaction it can create in you – mental or physical.

Figure 3 is a list of fears. Read through it and write in your notebook any that apply to you. As you do this, also write a brief statement of how each fear holds you back. You may need to think about this for a while before you come up with the answer. Let's look at some examples first to give you an idea of what is required.

♦ 'One of my fears is *failure* and it holds me back from aiming for what I really want in life.'
♦ 'One of my fears is *disapproval* and it often holds me back from speaking my mind and saying what I really think.'
♦ 'One of my fears is *loss of financial security* and it holds me back from changing my job which I hate.'

> If you are to deal successfully with your fears it is very important that you get to the bottom of what your *real* fear is, otherwise you are in danger of trying to tackle the wrong area.

If you think you fear making phone calls ask yourself whether you're afraid of making *all* phone calls or just *some* phone calls. If it is just *some* phone calls, which ones? It may turn out that you are only afraid of making phone calls at work – your job is in tele-sales and what you *really* fear is rejection. It is not unusual for someone in such a situation to project this fear on to *all* telephone calls so that they eventually dread picking up the phone to make a call. By understanding this you can deal with the real fear, which is not making phone calls, but *rejection.*

Try it now   Write in your notebook any of the fears in Figure 3 that apply to you together with a brief statement of how they hold you back. Add any additional fears that you may have.

Dealing with your fears

In any group of people you would probably be surprised how many things each person fears. There are also some very common fears that people share – loss of financial security, disapproval, being alone. You are not alone in your fears!

Rest assured you are already on the way to dealing with them. So what happens next? How can you get rid of each of your fears? Do you want to get rid of them all? Sometimes you may feel that it is more realistic to learn to deal with the fear and use it to your advantage than get rid of it. That might sound like strange advice, but look at it this way. Fear is sometimes a natural part of growing – the fear of meeting new people, trying new things, changing jobs, etc. As long as you want to continue to grow as a person you need to accept that fear will be a part of this process. By acknowledging this you should find it easier to live with it. The fear will become a natural step in your growth, not a barrier to it, thus you need not waste time and energy worrying about it because you know it is short-lived and will soon pass.

> Acknowledging your fears is the first step to dealing with them. Understanding how they hold you back is the next step.

One of my fears is...	...and it holds me back from:
Ageing	
Appearing weak	
Being alone	
Being assertive	
Being interviewed	
Children leaving home	
Change	
Changing career	
Disapproval	
Dying	
Ending a relationship	
Expressing my feelings	
Failure	
Gaining weight	
Illness	
Intimacy	
Loss of financial security	
Loss of image	
Losing a loved one	
Making decisions	
Making a mistake	
Making phone calls	
Meeting people	
Public speaking	
Rape	
Rejection	
Retirement	
Starting a relationship	
Success	

Fig. 3. A list of fears that might hold you back.

It's a bit like learning to ride a horse – you may be a bit afraid the first time you get on its back and the horse moves, but you know it's the only way you are going to learn to ride. Another good piece of news is that by confronting the thing you fear rather than avoiding it you will often feel so much better afterwards.

> Think about what you would have missed out on if you had failed to push through your fear.

Susan Jeffers, in her excellent book, *Feel the Fear and Do It Anyway,* makes a very interesting and relevant observation.

'Pushing through fear is less frightening than living with the underlying fear that comes from a feeling of helplessness.'

If you take this in, and really believe it, then pushing through your fear becomes a far more attractive proposition.

So, let's look at ways you can deal with the fears you wrote down in the last exercise – ways that will help you get rid of some of them and acknowledge that others are always going to be there as long as you continue to grow. For each fear that you wrote down, ask yourself the following questions:

(a) Where and when did this fear originate?

(b) What fuels this fear?

(c) How would your life be better if you didn't have this fear?

then

(a) Bombard the fear with logic.

(b) Deal with it one step at a time.

Let's examine these points in more detail:

Where and when did this fear originate?

You may or may not be able to remember the event that triggered your fear – it might even have evolved gradually. Try very hard. Ask someone else if you need to because this is often the key to understanding it. Was it something someone said or did? Who? When? What happened? Was it something you saw or read about rather than experiencing it personally?

How long have you held this fear? Has it grown stronger over time? Try to understand as much detail as you can about how this fear originated.

What fuels this fear?

Think about the life you lead now. Is there something in your life – an event, a person, a place, etc. – that keeps the fear alive and keeps fuelling it? For example, if you have a fear of disapproval, and your job involves chasing up customers who have not paid their bills, there is a fair chance your job is putting you in a position that fuels your fear. You are constantly having to face disapproval.

By understanding what it is that fuels your fear you are again putting yourself in a position where you can begin to do something about it.

How would your life be better if you didn't have this fear?

Try to imagine how your life would improve if you did not suffer from this fear. To help you, refer back to what you said the fear *prevented* you from doing and imagine how you would feel if you were *no longer* prevented from doing it. What about other related things – your self-esteem, your confidence, etc. – would they benefit too if you did not suffer with this fear?

Bombard the fear with logic

Many fears are irrational and illogical – if they were not then everyone would suffer them to the same degree. Fear is subjective. No two people experience fear in exactly the same way because no two people are the same. However, overcoming fear is not quite as simple as being able to say '*Well, it's irrational so I shouldn't be afraid...!*'

Bombard it with logic. To do this you need to play devil's advocate. Ask yourself some probing questions about it and look at some relevant facts.

- ◆ '*Other people aren't afraid of... so why should I be?*'
- ◆ '*If I push through the fear the worst thing that could happen is...?*'
- ◆ '*So what if I make a fool of myself – it's not the end of the world.*'

◆ *'If I get it wrong I can ask for help and try again.'*

Do this until you have convinced yourself that the fear is irrational and that you have no reason to go on suffering because of it. Get angry with it if it helps! Think about other people who appear not to have this fear – what's the difference between them and you? What can you learn from them?

Deal with it one step at a time

Once you have made up your mind to tackle the fear, don't feel that you have to overcome it all at once. If you have been afraid of something for years it's unlikely that you can get rid of the fear overnight. Instead think very carefully about what you need to do to overcome it. Think in *stages*, small steps. 'First I need to... once I've done that I can... then...'

To help you, think back over everything that you have learned so far in this book. Go back and reread any chapters that you think will help you. Perhaps make this the first small step in helping you to overcome the fear.

You should find as you progress you begin to feel stronger and often you can tackle the last few steps all at once. Taking the initial step requires the most courage – but remember, if you love yourself then you will believe you deserve to sort it out in order to have the life you want.

Example

'One of my fears is being alone and it holds me back from ending my present unhappy relationship.'

Where and when did this fear originate?

'It originated when I was a teenager – about sixteen years old – and all my friends had steady boyfriends but I didn't. Then they all got engaged or married and I still didn't have a steady boyfriend – just a stream of short-term relationships.'

What fuels this fear?

'My fear of being alone is fuelled because all of my friends have got

*partners. If I end my current relationship I'm afraid that I won't
have anyone to go out with and so I'll be stuck at home on my own.
If I don't go out I won't meet new people so I won't be able to start
a new relationship and I'll end up having a lonely life.'*

How would your life be better if you didn't have this fear?

*'If I didn't have this fear of being alone I would end the
relationship. My life would be better because I would no longer
have to put up with my partner's unreliability, arguments, lies –
all of which leave me feeling angry or pretty worthless. It would
also give me the opportunity to try to find a happy relationship
with someone else.'*

Now bombard your fear with logic. Ask yourself whether all
your friends really do have partners or are you exaggerating?
Will they suddenly stop being your friends if you don't have a
partner? What are the advantages of ending this relationship –
where is it going? Have all your friends got *happy* relationships,
or are they in the same situation as you? If a friend was in the
situation you're in you would probably advise her to end the
relationship – so why don't you take your own advice? Surely
you'd be happier on your own than continuing with this
unhappy relationship?

Now you are in a position to deal with your fear one step at
a time. The first small step might be to list all the advantages
of ending the relationship – really think carefully about them. *'I
could learn to speak Italian which I've wanted to do for years –
and if I do that I'll meet new people'. 'Once I get over the pain I
should be much happier and less stressed.' 'It will give me the
opportunity to meet someone else who I can have a meaningful
relationship with before too many more years tick by'. 'I'll feel
better about myself because my boyfriend won't be constantly
criticising me and lying to me.'*

Once you've taken this first step and you're happy that the
advantages are worth ending the relationship for, you will have
a clearer idea of the next step. It's up to you how you tackle
this – for some situations you might prefer to think of all the
steps before you begin so you have a *start-to-finish* plan. For
others you might prefer to literally do it a step at a time and let
the next step evolve once you see how the first one turns out.

However, generally speaking it is best to have the overall plan mapped out first to give you a goal to aim for. The danger of not doing this is that you will give up along the way.

The next step might be to think about what you are going to say to your partner – what words are you going to use? Where and when are you going to do it? What is his reaction likely to be and how are you going to handle it? Do you want to remain friends, if possible, or not? In other words, think it through thoroughly, then go ahead and do it.

Making a checklist

Whenever you find yourself in a situation where there is a problem you need to tackle someone about, use Figure 4 as your checklist. It should help you to think through what you want to say. Making a checklist will help you to understand the process you need to follow. It is not only useful for solving problems, but can be used in any scenario when you need to think and plan what you are going to say in order to achieve your desired outcome. Figure 5 on page 149 is an example of what a completed checklist might look like.

How to use your checklist

1. **Name**

   Write down the name of the person with whom you have the issue or problem.

2. **Problem/issue**

   Describe the exact issue or problem. Make sure you are clear in your own mind what it is.

3. **Desired outcome**

   What do you want to happen as a result of your discussion? How do you want it to end up? Visualise your desired outcome. Remember to aim for a *win-win* situation – no one should come away from the meeting feeling they have lost.

1. Name:	
2. Problem/issue:	
3. Desired outcome:	
4. Fallback situation:	
5. When:	
6. Where – my territory or his/hers:	
7. My side of the desk or his/hers:	
8. Appropriate behaviours:	
9. How will I begin:	
10. How will he respond:	
11. How will I handle the response:	
12. How might I mess it up:	
13. How can I avoid messing it up:	

Fig. 4. Checklist.

4. Fallback situation

Meetings with people do not always turn out the way you want, no matter how good the planning! You may find you need to have a *fallback situation*, one which although it is not your desired outcome you would be prepared to accept. E.g. if you are going to ask your boss for a £50 a week pay rise your fallback situation might be that you are prepared to accept £25 a week. However, a word of caution! Do *not* go into the meeting with the fallback situation (£25) in the forefront of your mind – if you do, that is very likely to be what you end up with! Think positive, think about what you really want and only if it is obvious you are not going to get this should you resort to your fallback situation.

In some situations there may only be *one* acceptable outcome, therefore there can be *no* fallback situation. E.g. if you are going to tackle a customer about non-payment of a bill, the only acceptable outcome might be payment of the bill. If this does not happen you may need to take legal proceedings, or refuse to supply any further goods. Take care though in a situation like this not to say things if you are not prepared to carry them through and accept the consequences. Do not threaten legal action if you have no intention of pursuing it. This only weakens your case and reduces the chance of reaching your desired outcome.

5. When?

The sooner you deal with the situation, the sooner it should be resolved and you can get on with your life. Always write down the earliest possible date or time in here. If you need to make a phone call to arrange this, do it *now*. Write it in your diary.

6. Where – my territory or his/hers?

You need to carefully weigh up the best place to meet for your discussion. For example, if it's a work problem, should you discuss it in the office or in a private place? Would you prefer to go to the other person, or would you prefer them to come to you? Which is likely to have the best outcome? Weigh up the best place for the discussion to take place.

7. My side of the desk or his/hers?

Where are you going to meet for your discussion? If there is a desk or table between you will this act as a barrier? Would you be better both sitting on the same side of the desk or table – or would it be better if there was no desk? Should you sit in the living room, in the kitchen, next to each other, opposite each other? Weight up all the options and think about which will be most appropriate as this will affect how comfortable you both feel. It may feel very awkward trying to have a private discussion with your partner, for example, across the kitchen table with the children around waiting for their tea.

8. Appropriate behaviours

Refer back to chapters three and four, in particular the list of behaviours you should use under active listening in Chapter 4. There is a fair chance that you will need to do some active listening if you are to hear what the other person has to say.

Think carefully about the list of influential behaviours in chapter three and which of these would be appropriate. Be aware too of any anti-influential behaviours you need to avoid!

> The important point here is to weigh up the most appropriate behaviours to use.

Should you take a gentle approach, or do you need to be firm? Do you need to be assertive in making your point, or do you need to ask an open question and let the other person do most of the talking? Because you know the person you will be talking to, and how they are likely to react, this puts you in a strong position to decide on the appropriate behaviours to use.

9. How will I begin?

This is your chance to think about and plan exactly what you are going to say – but don't let it sound like you are reading from a script! The way you start the discussion could well hold the key to how it turns out, so spend as much time as you need getting this bit right. Always remember that one of the most influential things to do is to be open and honest.

Often it is best to explain to the other person what the issue or problem is that you want to discuss. *'I'm concerned about the fact that I haven't received any payment yet for the work I did for you two months ago...'* or *'I'd like to talk to you about the argument we had last week. I don't feel we reached an amicable solution and it hurts me that we're having to avoid each other...'*

Present the *facts*, state how you *feel*, but do not criticise or blame the other person as this will only serve to make matters worse. Practise what you are going to say until you are sure it feels right. Remember the techniques you learned for being assertive and use them if necessary – turn back to chapter seven and reread it if you need to.

10. How will he or she respond?

Ask yourself – *'If I start like this, how will the other person respond?'* If you know the other person, you will have a fairly good idea how they will respond. Think of all the different ways they could respond. Try not to leave any avenues uncovered as this will help you to deal with the response.

11. How will I handle the response?

You need to think carefully about how you will react to the other person's response. Once again, try to plan how you will react to all of the possible responses. Sometimes it can be very effective to simply repeat what you said earlier. This serves to reinforce your point.

12. How might I mess it up?

Know your strengths, know your weaknesses. If you tend to shout and get angry, this may foul things up. If you are too timid and apologise for what you say, this, too, might mess it up.

13. How can I avoid messing it up?

Often, being aware of how you might mess it up can prevent you from doing so. If you know you normally shout and lose your temper, think very carefully about how you can prevent yourself from doing this. You have done a lot of work throughout the book on getting rid of anti-influential

1. Name:	*My partner.*
2. Problem/issue:	*I am unhappy in our relationship – my partner is unreliable and often lies to me.*
3. Desired outcome:	*End the relationship amicably.*
4. Fallback situation:	*None. However it may end up un-amicably, but I will do whatever I can to prevent this.*
5. When:	*Tonight.*
6. Where – my territory or his/hers:	*At my house – when he comes to pick me up.*
7. My side of the desk or hers:	*In the front room, sitting in adjacent armchairs.*
8. Appropriate behaviours:	*Remain calm, but assertive. Explain that I want to finish the relationship and why – tell him how it makes me feel.*
9. How will I begin:	*'It's been worrying me for some time now that our relationship doesn't seem to be making either of us happy...'*
10. How will he/she respond:	*He might interrupt me and try to say it's not his fault. Or he might deny that he's unhappy.*
11. How will I handle the response:	*Stay calm. Ask him to please let me finish what I want to say. Give him the facts about why I'm unhappy, e.g. his unreliability, but don't sound as if I'm blaming him – tell him how his behaviour makes me feel.*
12. How might I mess it up:	*By letting him persuade me to give the relationship another try. Or I might lose my temper.*
13. How can I avoid messing it up:	*Keep thinking about all the positive reasons for ending the relationship, and how much better I will feel once I have done it. Rehearse what I want to say and count to ten before I respond – this should help me to avoid losing my temper.*

Fig. 5. An example of a completed checklist.

behaviours and becoming more influential – now is the time to put it into practice.

Try it now	1. Take one of your fears and use the above process to work out a way of dealing with it. If appropriate, use the checklist to help you and write your responses in your notebook.
	2. When you have done this, take the first small step.

It can sometimes help to talk through your fear – and your feelings about the fear – with someone you trust. Not only does it give you the opportunity to voice your feelings, but it also opens up the possibility of finding someone else to help you in your quest to overcome it.

Exploring the advantages of dealing with your fears

Once you start to face up to your fears and deal with them you should find that there are many advantages to be gained:

◆ Life as a whole becomes more enjoyable because you are not ruled by fear.
◆ Your outlook on life becomes more positive.
◆ You feel more confident.
◆ You have higher self-esteem.
◆ You will laugh at yourself for being afraid.
◆ You will set an example to others and may be able to help them overcome some of their fears.
◆ You will be able to accept fear as a normal part of growing – rather than letting it rule your life.

Summary

In chapter eight you have seen how fear can prevent you from getting what you want out of life. You now know a process for facing up to your fears and dealing with them:

◆ Where and when did this fear originate?
◆ What fuels this fear?
◆ How would your life be better if you didn't have this fear?
◆ You then need to bombard the fear with logic.
◆ And deal with it one step at a time.

CHAPTER 9

Rebuilding the New You

Within us all, whoever we may be, regardless of how big a success or failure we think we are, is the ability and power to do whatever we need to do in order to be happy and successful.

> Within you right now is the power do things you never dreamed possible.

Recognising your strengths as well as your weaknesses will contribute immeasurably towards understanding your true capabilities and having a better life. These final three chapters will help you make the choices that will build a new and better future.

At the start of this book we said that happiness could be yours, day in and day out, and as you journeyed through the book you did exercises and learned techniques to help remove any blocks that were holding you back. This chapter builds on the earlier work you have done, pulling it together to help build your self-esteem by focusing on your achievements and your successes. In turn, this will help you rid yourself of any doubts or negative feelings you may still have about yourself. This may not happen overnight but the time and effort you put in will pay tremendous dividends in helping you get in touch with your real worth and value.

Exploring the things that can hold you back

Earlier in the book you read about how past conditioning can affect your self-esteem and consequently hold you back. Because of their past conditioning many people:

◆ Do not value themselves properly
◆ Do not love themselves enough.
◆ Are embarrassed to talk about their achievements.

- ◆ Underrate themselves and sell themselves short.
- ◆ Let negative thoughts and feelings suppress positive thoughts and feelings.

> Far too many people are willing to talk about their failures, but not their successes.

Do you ever find yourself falling into this habit? Any negative concept you have about yourself can prevent you working through your fears and can stop you from taking risks which are necessary if you are to develop and grow as a person.

In this chapter you will discover the power of giving yourself *I can...* messages instead of *I can't...* messages.

Writing your success chart

Writing down your successes will give you a visual record of the things you've achieved in your life so far. Then if the *doubter* inside tells you that you can't do something you can read through your list of successes and remind yourself that you have achieved many things in the past and that there's no reason why you shouldn't continue to do so in the future! This has proved to be a very powerful pick-me-up for many people and has repaid the effort involved.

> The first step in rebuilding the new you is to identify and write down your successes.

We have found that an enjoyable way of recording your successes and helping you to remember them is to divide your life into thirds and think about the successes you enjoyed in each third of your life. Before we explain how to do this, please remember what you have learned throughout this book about the word *success*. It is a subjective word – something that is personal to you and which may mean something totally different to each person who reads this book. In broad terms, it is a word that is used to describe something beneficial or worthwhile that you have achieved or accomplished in your life.

> Do not think that you need to have achieved something great in order to include it in your list of successes.

For many people a success can be something ordinary, but which produced a sense of achievement at the time – like learning to walk, or swim, or ride a bicycle, or passing your driving test. The main thing is to realise how important it was to you and remember how good it felt at the time. Think also about how different your life would be if you hadn't achieved each success – if you couldn't walk or talk for example, or if you hadn't passed your exams or got married or had children...

Recalling early successes

Breaking your life down into thirds should help you to remember the various successes that you have enjoyed *throughout* your life. It can be easy to forget that successes happen all the time – some large, some small – and you may find you have a tendency to forget or play down what you did in your earlier life and concentrate on more recent events. This exercise asks you to think about the successes you have had throughout your life, and in doing so remember the feelings you experienced at the time, the sense of achievement.

It is important to write down the things that you personally consider to have been successes. It doesn't matter that other people might have different ideas about whether they qualify as successes or not! This exercise is about *you*.

Early successes in Figure 6 include learning to walk and to ride a bicycle. You may laugh and consider that these aren't particularly significant achievements. But the important point is that at the time these were big achievements in a young life. Just because walking and riding a bicycle are common achievements for many people doesn't make the original achievement any less of a success. So if you find yourself struggling to think of successes in any of the thirds of your own life, keep this point in mind and don't tone down any of your achievements. Without them you wouldn't be able to do many of the things you can do today.

Try it now This is an opportunity for you to compile your own success chart. We will take you through the process step by step. Copy the success chart in Figure 6 into your notebook and follow the instructions below.

SUCCESS CHART

Age: 51

Divide your age by three: 17

For each third of your life write down as many successes a you can think of:

First third	1. *Learning to walk.*
	2. *Learning to ride a bicycle.*
0 – 17	3. *Passing the News of the World cycling proficiency test.*
Second third	1. *Becoming a father for the first time.*
	2. *Becoming a high performing sales manager and consequently qualifying to attend a sales convention in Bermuda.*
18 – 34	3. *Helping to build up and run a branch of the Samaritans in London.*
Third third	1. *Being appointed Head of Management Development for a fast growing life assurance company.*
	2. *Setting up my own business and making it a successful enterprise.*
35 – 51	3. *Taking a trip to New York on Concorde.*

Fig. 6. An example of a success chart.

Step 1

Divide your age by *three* – this will break down your life into thirds. Write down the resulting number of years.

Using Frank as an example, he is 51, so after dividing 51 by 3 the result is 17 years. Do not worry if you end up with a fraction rather than a whole year – e.g. if you are 31, then $31 \div 3 = 10^1/_3$ – use the fraction, or round it up to 11 or down to 10, whichever you prefer.

Step 2

Write down as many successes as you can remember from each third of your life. Ensure you have enough space to write up to three successes from each third of your chart although this does not mean you are limited to just three. Figure 6 is an example of a completed success chart. Read this before attempting to complete your own.

Completing your success chart should have helped you start focusing on your successes and have opened your mind to the fact that you have been more successful than you probably care to admit.

> Often, because people don't talk about their successes, they tend to let them take a back seat and, when remembering them, pass over them as being trivial.

You will find that it has a far more positive effect, both mentally and physically, if you keep these successes in your mind and think about them regularly. Tell yourself that no matter what else has happened in your life you have succeeded in all of these things.

Logging your day-to-day achievements

Having reflected on your past successes it's important to maintain the success momentum and let it drive you forward. To help you do this, it helps to write down at least one thing that you achieve each and every day of your life. Some days your achievement may be comparatively small and seemingly mundane like clearing out the clutter from your bedroom or office or kitchen. Other days you might achieve something greater: *'I was offered a job – ten people had been short-listed, but they selected me.'* Great or small, it helps you to focus on things you have done that have got *results*.

What if there are no achievements?

If there are days when you feel you haven't achieved anything worth writing down, stop and think again about what you have done and what you have achieved – there should always be something. However, if you find that a feeling of non-achievement prevails, we recommend you take time out to review how you are spending your days. Try to discover what is creating the feeling of non-achievement. You have covered much in this book so far about overcoming negative and destructive influences in your life, and in the remaining chapters you will find out even more about this. Choosing a better life is about feeling motivated and fulfilled, and an important component is feeling that the things you do each day are worthwhile. If some things you do are not worthwhile, you must ask yourself why you continue to do them, because as long as you do so you will continue to feel demotivated and unfulfilled.

Writing it all down

For some people the power of this exercise is so great that they buy a special book in which to record each day's achievements. Others write it in their diary. It's up to you, but the important thing is to write it down where you can easily refer to it.

> Logging your achievements helps you to replace I can't messages with I can messages.

If there is still a negative, doubtful voice inside, it should start to fade away and a new positive voice should appear in its place. Over the days, weeks, months and years that lie ahead you will find that you build up a potent record of the things you have achieved.

Whenever you feel in need of reassurance, stop what you are doing. Read through your success chart and your list of day-to-day achievements and remind yourself of all the things you have achieved. This can work particularly well when:

◆ You are feeling low or having a bad day.
◆ You need a confidence boost.
◆ You are about to embark on something new and feel a bit nervous.
◆ You are feeling demotivated and finding it hard to get going.

Once you get into the habit of writing down your daily achievements it should not only become enjoyable but should also help focus your mind on the positive things that happen all the time, which in turn helps to give you a more positive perspective on life.

Cultivating good habits

Keeping a record of your achievements is a habit that should have a positive outcome or effect. However, not all habits are good ones! One area that can hold back the new you is your old habits – the things you do routinely without really thinking too much about why.

> In order to move forward in rebuilding the new you, you need to check out your habits and see if there are any you need to change.

For example, you may have a habit of watching television every night regardless of what is on. Sitting down at seven o'clock every night in front of the television, your meal on your lap, watching whatever is on the screen and then wondering where the night has gone. That's fine if it makes you happy and it gives you pleasure and relaxation or stimulation. But it's not fine if it leaves you feeling frustrated, bored and unfulfilled. If this is the case, start a new habit to replace the current one. Do something you are going to enjoy, even if it's something as simple as eating your meal at the table away from the television and then going for a walk or reading a book. Highlight the television programmes you *want* to watch, but find something else to do when these are not on. The important thing is to break the bad habit and do something fulfilling.

It is not the aim of this book to pass judgment on what are good or bad habits. This is something that you must decide for yourself, perhaps with some help from your family, friends and work colleagues who are best placed to help you identify these. Remember, bad habits often go hand in hand with the anti-influential behaviours you looked at in chapters three and four. The important thing if you are to have a better life is to review your habits. Keep the ones you are happy with and change the ones you are not happy with.

Try it now   To help you begin the process of change make a list in your notebook of any of your own habits that you would like to break, and consider the benefits of doing so.
For example:
'I would like to break the habit of watching television for four hours every night – even when there are no good programmes.' 'The benefits of breaking this habit are that I could do more enjoyable and productive things like reading, spending time with the children or catching up on my accounts. This would make me feel better and more fulfilled.'

Thirty days to make or break a habit

In Chapters 10 and 11 you will do some more work in this area, taking it a step further by planning to do the things you *want* to do in your life.

We have often heard people say that bad habits are easy to fall into and get stuck with but good habits are not so easy to cultivate. Yet if, as some research shows, it takes 30 days to establish a habit then logically that is how long it should take to break any bad ones and replace them with good ones. 30 days from *now* you could have broken your bad habits. In the grand scale of life 30 days is a comparatively tiny amount of time! True, the first 30 days are likely to be the worst, as many people who have given up smoking will testify. But if you can get through those 30 days there is a very strong likelihood that the old, bad habit will be broken.

It is easier to break an old habit by replacing it with a new one. Sadly there are many people who get themselves into a rut, doing the same old things day after day, and consequently miss out on much of life's rich tapestry.

> Rebuilding the new you is all about becoming happier and more successful doing what you *want* to do.

Look at how many people become mature students in order to gain further education or a degree they missed out on in their younger life. The studying can be hard, but once it becomes a habit it generally becomes easier to do and more enjoyable. And, what is more, it brings the reward of a sense of achievement and a feeling of success.

Using feedback to rebuild the new you

When people fall into bad habits they tend to justify these habits to themselves without considering or realising the impact they can have on other people. For example, what is the impact on their family of sitting slumped in front of the television every night?

Similarly, many people fail to realise the positive effect that their good habits can have on others. Habits like holding doors open for other people or always saying please when you ask someone to do something.

Another powerful tool in rebuilding the new you is feedback. Feedback from other people on the impact *your behaviour* or *your habits* have on them. To help build an awareness of both the positive and negative impact these can have, feedback from other people is vital. In chapter two you learned that one of the six basic principles for building a better life is to *give people descriptive feedback to help them develop*. Read through this again now if you need to refresh your memory.

For the purposes of this chapter *behaviour* falls into two categories:

◆ Behaviour which is influential and which you should *keep*.
◆ Behaviour which is anti-influential and which you should *change*.

Your behaviour is what often has the greatest impact on people.

They will form their opinion of you based on your behaviour, and behaviour can easily become a habit – good or bad.

As you have already discovered, your behaviour may not always have the impact you intend. You might think you are being funny when you make a joke about your friend's new skinhead haircut, but your friend might find your comments – and thus your behaviour – humiliating. Remember the example in chapter four about the sales manager whose sarcasm had a very different effect to the one he intended? Unless someone *tells* you about the impact – positive or negative – of your behaviour on them, you may never know and thus never have the opportunity to do something about it.

You now have the opportunity to receive some feedback about the impact of your behaviour on other people, which can help you move one step closer to having a better life. You may already have touched on this when you considered your influential and anti-influential behaviours in chapters three and four, however there is even greater benefit to be gained by seeking descriptive feedback from other people.

Exercise
This exercise involves other people – because you cannot build a better life if you have a poor interpersonal relationship with someone who is a regular part of your life, whether at work or at home. It can help you to understand the impact that your behaviour has on those around you.

Part 1
Think about the people with whom you have regular contact and those with whom it is important that you have a good interpersonal relationship. Of these, select the ones whose feedback you believe would be useful to you and valuable in helping you determine the impact your behaviour has.

Initially you may wish to limit the number of people you ask for feedback – try to get enough to give you a reasonable spread covering all the main areas of your life (home, work, social, etc). This will give you a strong basis on which to begin to assess your impact. However, feedback should be an ongoing process and ideally you need to build up to the point where you feel comfortable asking people for it. It will not always be necessary, or appropriate, to write it down, but often a simple question like 'What did I do or say?' will encourage feedback once people get into the habit and feel comfortable giving it. Good, descriptive feedback is vital to help you develop and grow and get the best out of your interpersonal relationships.

In your notebook, write down the names of up to ten people who you would initially like to give you feedback.

Part 2

Approach each of these people *individually*. Explain that you would welcome any feedback they are prepared to give which will help you understand the impact you have on others and which will help you become more influential. Remember to explain to each person that you need to know how your behaviour impacts on *them* personally – not how they think it impacts on other people. Second-hand feedback, or guessing, is not what you are looking for.

Try to put them at ease about giving this feedback. If they don't feel comfortable then you will gain little benefit, and they may end up feeling that they have let you down. Explain that you will simply *listen* to what they have to say – you will not agree or disagree with them as that is not the purpose of the exercise. You will only speak if you need to clarify something they say.

Explain that you would like descriptive feedback on:

◆ Any of your behaviours which they personally find *influential* and which you should *keep*.
◆ Any of your behaviours which they personally find *anti-influential*, which you need to *change* in order to have a greater influence or a better impact on them.

It is important to make the feedback *descriptive* and *constructive*, otherwise you can end up feeling as though you are being judged or criticised. If this happens, the whole exercise will leave you feeling negative rather than positive so let's spend a bit of time now reiterating the important points about *how* the feedback should be given in order to be effective and beneficial.

By asking the people who give you feedback to give it in the following style you should find that this is an enormous help in making it descriptive and constructive and it will give you something meaningful to work on.

(a) Keep feedback

When giving feedback on any behaviours which they find *influential* and which you should therefore *keep*, encourage them to use wording like: '*I find your*... (specify behaviour) *influential because*...(briefly describe why – how does it make them feel?).'

For example, '*I find your positive attitude influential because it makes me feel that I should try to see the positive side of things too instead of always finding fault.*' Or '*I find your honesty very influential because I know that whenever I ask you something you will give me an honest answer, and that makes me feel I can trust you.*'

The person giving the feedback should try to avoid saying things like '*I like it when you smile*', or '*I think you're honest*'. This is not particularly helpful because it doesn't clarify the *impact* that your behaviour has on the other person or why it is influential. Try to encourage them to say more by asking open questions like '*What makes you say that?*' '*How does it make you feel?*' Unless you have this sort of detail you may not understand the full strength of your influential behaviour.

(b) Change feedback

When giving feedback on any behaviours which they find *anti-influential*, and which you should consider *changing* if you want to have a greater influence or better impact on them, encourage them to use wording like: '*You would have a greater influence on me if you*...(specify anti-influential behaviour that needs to change). *When you*... (specify anti-influential behaviour) *it makes me*...(describe how it makes you feel, or the effect it has on you).'

For example '*You would have a greater influence on me if you did not get aggressive when you disagree with something I've said. When you get aggressive it makes me feel intimidated and angry. I feel like a naughty child and that makes me want to argue with you instead of talking through the issue sensibly*', or '*When you agree with everything I say it gives me the impression that you lack the confidence to say what you really believe. You would have a greater influence on me if you didn't always agree with me.*' Note the choice of words in this example: '*...it gives me the impression that you lack the confidence...*' This is what is important for you to hear – the *impression* or *impact* your behaviour has on that person. This is very different from saying '...it *shows* that you lack confidence...' Comments like this, however well-intentioned, can appear judgmental and critical and can encourage you to retort or become defensive.

Good descriptive feedback simply states *facts* and *feelings*. At no time does it pass judgment on your behaviour. This is crucial, because if the other person appears to be passing judgment on you, or telling you how you should behave, this can make you defensive. If it happens, gently encourage the person giving the feedback to say it differently. For example, 'It would help me understand more if you could explain how it makes you feel when I do that. Tell me why you find this behaviour anti-influential.'

Part 3

As you receive the feedback – both keep *and* change – write it down in your notebook. This is to help you remember what has been said so that you can give it your full consideration afterwards. You should not interrupt while the feedback is being given, other than to question anything you are not clear about or to say thank you at the end. Whatever you do, *do not* defend or justify your anti-influential behaviour by making excuses like 'I'm not normally like that.' 'No one else feels like that about it.' At the same time don't dismiss your influential behaviour by playing it down, saying things like 'It's nothing really... Other people do it better...' Remember that what you are hearing from the other person is the *impact* your behaviour has on him or her.

Using the feedback constructively

When you have received the *keep and change* feedback from your selected group of people, read through it again and make sure you understand it.

> The keep feedback will help you understand what you do that has a positive influence on other people.

It will enable you to build on it in order to have an even

greater influence – with new acquaintances as well as existing ones. It's also good to read through this from time to time, particularly if you are feeling a bit low. In many ways it has the same effect as your success chart – it focuses on the positive things about you. You may not have realised how great your impact on other people is. The *keep* feedback will clarify or reinforce this, particularly if the same feedback has been given by more than one person. It is telling you that these are some of your strengths. By acknowledging this and building on these strengths it will help you find the balance that works best in your interpersonal relationships.

The *change* feedback is a very powerful tool for helping you to understand why some of the things you do have a negative impact, and how this can cause you problems with other people or stop you getting the reactions you desire. Pay particular attention to any anti-influential behaviours that have been commented on by more than one person. The more people who give the same feedback, the stronger the negative effect of your behaviour is likely to be. For example, if six out of eight people tell you that your swearing is anti-influential, the more negative and widespread the effect is, and the greater the need to decide whether you are going to do anything about it.

> Just as the keep feedback pointed out your strengths, the change feedback is pointing out areas of weakness in your interpersonal relationships.

You may or may not have been aware of this before and may have wondered why sometimes you didn't have the impact you intended!

Having weighed up the *change* feedback, the choice is *yours* whether or not to do anything about it. It will have told you how your anti-influential behaviours can have a negative impact on the people around you. It is now up to you to weigh up the pros and cons of continuing with the same behaviour and living with the consequences or changing it in order to have a more positive influence or impact.

How to handle conflicting feedback

You may find that you receive conflicting feedback from people. For example, one person might say your sense of humour is funny and very influential while another might say it is inappropriate and anti-influential.

Remember to ask for clarification if you are not sure what each piece of feedback means. But be careful not to justify or defend it, or argue against it. Once you are sure you understand the feedback, think about what each person has said, and why your behaviour affected individuals differently. Perhaps it was the circumstances at the time that caused the differing feedback. For example, maybe your humour *was* appropriate and funny when you made a witty comment at work, but it was taken as being sarcastic and critical when you said the same thing to your partner at home.

By becoming aware of issues like this you can choose whether to make changes to your behaviour in different areas of your life. Keep your sense of humour at work because your colleagues find it funny but do not use it at home if you want to have a more positive impact and avoid causing offence or upset.

You may even find that there is an underlying problem that needs sorting out – *why* does your partner at home get upset and feel you are being critical? Perhaps there is a hidden agenda, or suppressed emotions? However, initially you should simply listen to the feedback and thank your partner for giving it. Afterwards, when you are weighing it up, you must decide whether you need to talk to your partner about it. You may find it helpful to refer back to chapter six on expressing feelings.

Surprise feedback

Most people are not surprised by the feedback they receive, particularly about their anti-influential behaviours. Consciously or subconsciously they are aware that something is not quite right! Occasionally you will receive a bit of feedback that *does* surprise you. It may well relate to a behaviour that has become so habitual you don't realise you are doing it, for example tugging your hair while you are speaking, or shifting about from one leg to the other. Although you are blind to what you are doing, the impact on the other person can be very irritating and anti-influential. It is important for you to *hear* about such an impact from other people. It is often this *hearing* that spurs you into doing something about it – as long as it remains unsaid it is easy to ignore! Only by heeding the change feedback and doing something about it can you hope to have a greater influence and more positive impact on the people around you. You will find that your life becomes so much richer when your interpersonal relationships are working well.

Summary

In this chapter you have started the process of rebuilding the new you. To help you do this you have:

- Revisited your successes from the past.
- Learned about keeping a record of your day-to-day achievements.
- Looked at how bad habits can be replaced with good habits in just thirty days.
- Received feedback on influential behaviours you should keep and anti-influential behaviours you may wish to change.

CHAPTER 10

Finding the Balance

Y ou have now reached the point where you can plan the life you want by balancing all the different areas of your lifestyle in a way that brings happiness and fulfilment.

There is no magic formula for the *right* balance because everyone is different. Also, the balance that feels right in your life *now* may not feel right in the future.

> People change, goals change, ideas change – all it means is that you may need to review and, if appropriate, adjust the balance to take into account any changes you want to make.

It's a bit like making a cake. One day you get all the ingredients weighed out, you follow the recipe, and you bake a mouth-watering fruit cake. However, next time you decide that you would prefer a chocolate cake. It's simply a case of weighing out a different set of ingredients and following the appropriate recipe to find the right mix for the chocolate cake. It won't necessarily be better or worse than the fruit cake – it's just different, and what you want at the time!

Life would be very boring if it stayed the same and never changed, wouldn't it – if you always had to eat fruit cake because that was what you originally decided you wanted!

Your responsibility, your choice

In this chapter you will be finding out *how* you can plan the life you want, and how to make any adjustments you need to make. Remember what has been said throughout this book. Your life is in *your* control and no one else's – other people may have an *influence*, but only you have control, and hence the choice of what to do. How you use this choice is up to you. If you are not happy with your life at the moment, or if you think some or all of it could be better, it's up to you to take the responsibility for doing something about it. Don't blame other people if you make the wrong choices or if you aren't prepared to take personal responsibility for making changes.

If you love, value and respect yourself surely you owe it to yourself to have the life you want. As you proceed through this chapter you will come across accounts of people who adjusted the balance in their lives and who are very much happier as a result – this includes the authors!

Your ideal day

How often do you hear people say 'There aren't enough hours in a day'? Have you ever said this yourself?

The fact is, there are 24 hours in a day, it's the same for everyone.

> It's how you choose to use these twenty-four hours that makes the difference between enjoying each day, getting through each day, or dreading each day.

If you *choose* to try to cram too many activities into your day *you* must take the responsibility for that choice and suffer the consequences – don't blame the day for not having enough hours in it!

To find the right balance for *your* life you first need to make sure that each day is filled with activities which are meaningful and which you enjoy. If not you will find that you are wasting negative energy in an effort to get through them. Finding the right balance also means not feeling guilty about time spent doing activities you want to do, particularly any relaxing activities like taking a full lunch hour or spending a quiet half hour reading the newspaper. This may entail asking someone else for their help, perhaps changing your job so that it fits in with what you want to do, or spending less time at work so that you can have more quality time at home.

> Achieving the right balance is about finding a way of making mundane activities more enjoyable, or finding an alternative way of getting them done.

Case Study _____

Nicola used to spend long hours, including Saturday mornings, working. Her work was taking over her life and left her feeling tired and flat when she got home. She enjoyed horse riding but had very little time to do it. Consequently she began to dislike her job and think about changing it.

After reviewing and adjusting the balance between work and home Nicola made some astonishing changes. She realised that in fact she enjoyed her job, but the number of hours she spent there was getting her down. So instead of working until nine o'clock most evenings she went home at five o'clock and at lunch time on a Friday – working Saturday mornings to compensate for this. In the time she gained by doing this she was able to ride her horse five times a week and enjoy it.

Her work didn't suffer as a result of spending fewer hours there. She simply found a more effective and productive way of doing her job, which in turn gave her greater motivation and satisfaction. Her productivity *increased* as a result of working less hours. She now enjoys her home life, loves her job and is one of the top performers in the country within the company she works for.

_____

There is no reason you cannot achieve similar results in your life if, like Nicola, you are prepared to make choices and take responsibility for doing something about them. We shall now look at how you can take the first step in this process. It concentrates on things you enjoy doing or would like to do and asks you to combine them into an *ideal day*.

Introduction to exercises

The next three exercises build up to form an overall blueprint for a better future. Each exercise is of equal importance in making this blueprint work.

Most people have to work to earn a living. If you are in this position your ideal day must contain an element of work sufficient to bring in the income you require. You may dream of having sufficient money not to need to work but in order to get there you first need to earn the money.

By focusing on the type of work you enjoy doing, or would like to do, in order to earn that sort of money, you are educating your mind to think in a positive way about your work. The aim of these exercises is to help you wake up each morning looking forward to the day because, in your present circumstances, it is the closest you can get to being an ideal day.

Therefore when you think about your ideal day in these exercises remember to include work if you need to, otherwise you will suffer constant disillusionment.

The instructions for the exercises relate to activities you would include in your ideal *working* day. However, you can repeat the exercises to cover weekends, days off, holidays, etc, where your ideal mix of activities will be different. Unless you know how you would like to spend your ideal day in all of these scenarios you stand little chance of ever achieving it.

To begin these exercises you may find it helps to relax, close your eyes, and actually visualise the things you would do on your ideal day – the clearer the picture you have, the easier it will be to do them. Start from the moment you wake up and slowly picture your day unfolding. Visualise yourself living your ideal day, doing the things you enjoy and enjoying the things you do. Experience the enjoyment, listen to the sounds, imagine the taste, the smell, the feel of things...right through to the time you go to sleep.

Instructions for Exercise 1

You will need to consider the following points *before* doing the exercise on page 172.

♦ Break your day down into as many *specific activities* as you can, e.g. *read* the paper, *telephone* three potential new customers. Avoid using expressions that cover a whole range of activities like *go to work*. Try to be more specific about the various activities you would do when you do *go to work*.

If you don't enjoy your work at the moment, write down the work you would ideally (and realistically) like to do. Remember this exercise is asking you to think about how your *ideal* day would be spent – this includes time spent at home before and after work.

♦ Only include activities that you want to happen on a *daily* basis – not those that happen *occasionally*.

♦ Try to include as many things as you can that you enjoy and that are important to you. This includes things like taking a full one hour lunch break or having a relaxing shower.

◆ Do not include things because you think you should – only write down things you want to have in your ideal day. You will find out how to deal with activities you don't enjoy but which you feel you *have* to do in Exercise 3.

◆ Your list may vary depending on the time of year you are writing it. For example, in summer you might include sunbathing, whereas it's unlikely to appear if you are writing your list in the winter!

◆ Do not write down how long you would spend doing each activity unless it is an integral part of that activity, e.g. take a full *one hour* lunch hour. The important thing for the moment is to write the *activity* down.

Before you have a go yourself, look at the example below to see how an *ideal day* activity list might look.

◆ Have a *relaxing* bath or shower.
◆ Go for a walk.
◆ Write minimum 10 pages for a self-development book or an article for a magazine.
◆ Write minimum 10 pages for novel.
◆ Marketing – contact existing and potential customers about work.
◆ Carry out research for books.
◆ Spend time in the garden relaxing or gardening.
◆ Read a book.
◆ Read a newspaper or magazine.
◆ Prepare and enjoy a nice evening meal.
◆ Housework (a bit each day).
◆ Watch an *interesting* television programme or video.
◆ Listen to music (possibly alongside other activities).

This list only includes activities to be done on a *daily* basis – it does not include occasional activities (like shopping, visiting publishers, editing books, go out for a drink or a meal, write letters, visit family or friends, etc). We will explain how to take into account these other activities later.

The important points is to be sure you will enjoy doing all of the activities. Don't put something on your list just because it's currently a part of your working life and you feel you *must*. Please keep this in mind when you are writing your own list.

Exercise 1	In your notebook, write down the activities that *you* would like to include in your own ideal (working) day.

When you have finished your list, read back over it and ask yourself how you would feel if you could spend each working day like this? If the answer is anything less than *great*, go back and review your list. What's wrong with it? Is there something missing, or something on there that you wouldn't really enjoy doing in your ideal day?

If necessary, amend your list before you read any further, until you feel you have got it right.

Instructions for Exercise 2

In Exercise 2 we are gong to take into account all of the *occasional* activities which are not on your *daily* list, but which you enjoy – or would like to enjoy – on a regular basis during your working week. For example, writing letters, placing orders with suppliers, going out for a drink in the evening, going shopping, etc. Let's think about these now, because even though they may not happen *daily* they do happen *regularly* – or you would like them to. Once again, when writing this list remember only to include activities you will *enjoy*.

Before you have a go yourself, have a look at the example below of a list of *occasional* activities (once again using the author as the example):

- ◆ Shopping.
- ◆ Washing and ironing.
- ◆ Networking with people I know to get more business or publicity.
- ◆ Reviewing business plan.
- ◆ Doing the book-keeping.
- ◆ Going for a drink or a meal.
- ◆ Writing letters.

Please note that these are all activities included as part of an ideal *working* week. By choosing to include shopping, washing and ironing this leaves weekends free to do other activities.

Exercise 2	In your notebook write down the *occasional* activities that *you* would include in your own ideal (working) day.

When you consider the time needed to slot in these occasional activities your ideal day will probably be looking reasonably full – even if part of it is filled by some time to relax and do nothing! The only things that should not be in there are those activities you do on a daily, or occasional, basis
· which you feel you *have* to do, but which you do not enjoy doing. You will be dealing with these next in Exercise 3.

Introduction to Exercise 3

Back to reality!

'It's okay saying that's how I'd like to spend my ideal day, but the reality is it's not that easy!'

How many of you are thinking this after completing Exercises 1 and 2? Our guess would be the majority of you. You may also feel inclined at this stage to point out that we have ignored a couple of important issues:

1. The above lists are things you would *like* to do – *desired activities* – they are not necessarily things you are doing now. Or maybe you are doing them, but not spending enough quality time doing them. For example, maybe you manage to have a quick shower and to flick through the newspaper before you go to work, but in your ideal day you said you would like to spend time *relaxing* when doing these activities.

2. The above lists ignore the things you are doing at the moment that you *don't* enjoy.

Let's address these two issues now because they are the areas that tend to cause disappointment, boredom, frustration or stress in our lives. Please keep in mind the following two points as you do the next part of the exercise:

1. The choice of what you do in your life is *yours* and yours alone. It may not always be an easy or a comfortable choice,

but only you can make it. Having made that choice, take responsibility for it – don't blame others if it is not what you want.

2. Are you prepared to pay the price for having what you want? This may involve making a sacrifice.

Incorporating desired activities into your ideal day

To begin with, look back at the activities you listed in your ideal day which you are *not* doing now or which you are not spending enough quality time doing. For each activity that falls into this category, ask yourself the following questions – be very honest with yourself when answering them:

1. Why have you included this activity in your ideal day – why is it so important to you?

2. Is it realistic and within your control to be able to do this activity?

3. How would your life have to change to enable you to do it?

4. Are you prepared to do whatever is necessary to bring this about?

5. Why aren't you currently doing it?

6. List three benefits to *you* of doing this every day.

Let's look at an example of how to use the above questioning technique to help you – we'll use *go for a walk* as the desired activity for this example:

1. **Why have you included this activity in your ideal day – why is it so important to you?**

   'I included it in my ideal day because it is important for my health and relaxation to take some daily exercise because my job is very sedentary. I enjoy walking and I am surrounded by some lovely countryside which I would like to see more of.'

2. **Is it realistic and within your control to be able to do this activity?**

'Yes, it is realistic and within my control. It is also free so it will not involve any expense.'

3. **How would your life have to change if you were to do it?**

'I would like to walk for 30 – 60 minutes daily so if I were to do it I would have to make the effort every day – this would involve sacrificing time currently spent doing other things. However, if I am honest I waste a lot of time so it's not really a great sacrifice – in fact it would be making much better use of my time.'

4. **Are you prepared to do whatever is necessary to bring this about?**

'Yes, I am prepared to make the effort and time.'

5. **Why aren't you currently doing it?**

'Because I can't be bothered to make the effort! Often it is easier just to slump in front of the television or read a magazine.'

6. **List three benefits to you of doing this every day.**

(a) *'I would feel fitter.'*

(b) *'It would get me out of the house or office for a while into the fresh air.'*

(c) *'I would see more of the countryside which will give me inspiration for my writing.'*

If, after asking yourself the above questions you are not convinced that you can do it you must ask yourself whether or not it should appear on your list. The danger of trying to include such an activity is that it can cause you stress or make you feel guilty if you fail to do it and that is something you could do without!

Instructions for Exercise 3

Once you are happy that your ideal day list contains only

176 Choosing a Better Life

activities that meet the above criteria, you are ready to move on to deal with those other activities – the ones that do not appear on your list but which you currently feel you *have* to do every day even though you don't enjoy them.

Begin by making a list of all such *daily* activities in your notebook. It will help if you can be specific about what it is that you don't enjoy. For example, rather than say *going to work* specify which part of your work you do not enjoy. By doing this you may find that you enjoy 80 per cent of what you do but the other 20 per cent is pulling you down.

Your list might include things like:

◆ Take the children to school and pick them up from school.
◆ Call on potential new customers.
◆ Cook a meal for the family each night.

Exercise 3   In your notebook write down the activities you do on a *daily* basis which you do not enjoy doing. When you have finished this, write down any *occasional* activities which you have to do, i.e. on an irregular basis, not necessarily daily but which you do *not* enjoy.

Dealing with activities you don't enjoy doing

Put simply, there are two options:

(a) Stop doing the activity.

(b) Find an alternative way of tackling the activity and make it more enjoyable.

> It is possible and within your control to get rid of the activities you don't enjoy.

The choice is yours! To help you make this choice, take each activity on your list in turn and ask yourself the following questions:

1. Why do you do this activity – what are the benefits?
   Warning – you are not allowed to answer this question by saying you do it because you have to or because it's your job! You need to get the real reason why you do it if you are to stand any chance of dealing with it effectively.

2. Why don't you enjoy doing this activity?

3. What can you do to make this activity more enjoyable?

4. Is there an alternative way of getting it done? List *all* the alternatives you can think of, also the advantages and disadvantages of each.

5. What would happen if you stopped doing this activity? Would you want this to happen?

6. Make your choice. Option (a) – *stop doing the activity*, or option (b) – *find an alternative way of tackling the activity or make it more enjoyable*. Specify exactly what you intend to do.

Let's look at some examples of how this questioning technique works.

Example 1

We'll start with *housework* and show you how one person used the above questioning technique to transfer this activity from her *have to do but don't enjoy* list to her *ideal day* list:

1. **Why do you do this activity – what are the benefits?**

   '*I do the housework to keep the house clean and tidy. The benefits are that the house looks great and I feel good about it. Mess and untidiness drains my energy, so an added benefit is that by keeping the house clean and tidy I feel constantly energised.*'

2. **Why don't you enjoy doing this activity?**

   '*Because it takes a lot of time to do it properly – I would rather be doing something else. Also it is messy – I feel like I need a shower when I have finished.*'

3. **What can you do to make this activity more enjoyable?**

   ◆ '*Focus on the benefits of doing it – clean and tidy house, energising, feels great once it's done, looks great if I have visitors – I don't feel ashamed of the mess!*'
   ◆ '*Do it a bit at a time instead of all at one.*'

◆ *'Play some music I enjoy while doing it.'*
◆ *'Reward myself when it's done (cup of tea, read the newspaper, etc).'*
◆ *'Have a shower when I've finished.'*

4. **Is there an alternative way of getting it done? List all the alternatives you can think of, plus the advantages and disadvantages of each.**

(a) *'I could pay a cleaner to do the housework. The advantage of that is that I would no longer have to do it myself and it would free up time to do more enjoyable and profitable things. The disadvantage is that I would have to pay for the cleaner's services which would use up some of my income and I am not sure if I would like anyone else doing such an intimate job.'*

(b) *'I could ask my husband to help me. The advantage of that is that I would have someone to share the work with me which would reduce my workload, and it might also make my husband keener to keep the house tidy in the first place! The disadvantage is that I would still have to do some of the housework myself, and I'm not sure that my husband's idea of cleaning and tidying the house is the same as mine!'*

(c) *'I could break it down into smaller chunks and do a bit each day rather than doing it all in one go once a week. This would make it less oppressive and less onerous, but it does mean that I will still have to do some or all of it myself.'*

5. **What would happen if you stopped doing this activity? Would you want this to happen?**

'If I stopped doing the housework the house would become dirty, messy and dusty. I would not want that!'

6. **Make your choice. Option (a) – stop doing the activity, or option (b) – find an alternative way of tackling the activity or make it more enjoyable. Specify exactly what you intend to do.**

'Option (b) has to be the one for me! I will achieve this by a combination of breaking it down into smaller chunks – doing a room each day, and also following the suggestions I have listed above for making it more enjoyable.'

Example 2

Here's how the questioning technique can be applied to another activity: calling on potential new customers.

1. **Why do you do this activity – what are the benefits?**

   '*I do it to try to get them to buy my products. The benefits are that if they buy my products I will increase my income because I will earn more commission. Also the more regular customers I can built up, the less cold calling I will need to do because I will earn sufficient commission from my regular customers.*'

2. **Why don't you enjoy doing this activity?**

   '*I get a lot of rejections – people can be very cold and rude sometimes. This can be demotivating – it often feels like I'm putting in a lot of effort for little reward. It knocks my confidence when I get a rejection and makes me wonder if I'm doing my job properly.*'

3. **What can you do to make the activity more enjoyable?**

   ◆ '*Analyse why I get rejections from some people and not others. This will help me to find alternative methods of approach.*'
   ◆ '*Don't take it personally when someone says no.*'
   ◆ '*Try to find a more effective way of selecting potential new customers – should I avoid certain types of people?*'
   ◆ '*Ask my manager to give me more feedback on my performance – he should be able to tell me if I am doing anything wrong and help me to do it more effectively.*'

4. **Is there an alternative way of getting it done? List all the alternatives you can think of, plus the advantages and disadvantages of each.**

   (a) '*Telephone potential customers rather than call on them personally. The advantage is that I will be able to contact far more people in a much shorter time and I can do this from the office or from home. The disadvantage is that telephone prospecting has a much lower success rate and I don't like doing it. Also I will not be able to show them my products or gauge their reactions.*'

(b) 'Concentrate more on my existing client base and try to get them to increase their orders. The advantage is that they already know me and my products and I feel much more at ease because I know the customers and their needs. The disadvantage is that this would leave me less time to find new customers – I still have targets to meet for bringing in new business.'

(c) 'Persuade my existing customers to give me referrals to people they know who might be interested in my products. The advantage is that I would find it easier to go in following a referral rather than cold and there is a greater chance of doing business if I have been recommended to them. The disadvantage is that my existing customers may get upset at being pressed for referrals (I have asked them before) and I am not very confident at asking for referrals – I tend to mess it up!'

5. **What would happen if you stopped doing this activity? Would you want this to happen?**

    'If I stopped calling on potential new customers I would have to rely on my existing customer base for my income – at the moment this is not as much as I would like to earn. Also I would not meet my targets for new business therefore I might lose my job. I wouldn't want that to happen.'

6. **Make your choice. Option (a) – stop doing the activity, or option (b) – find an alternative way of tackling the activity or make it more enjoyable. Specify exactly what you intend to do.**

    'I don't want to lose my job because I enjoy it, so it has got to be option (b). I will begin by following all of my suggestions for making the job more enjoyable, then once I have done this and analysed where I could do better, I will agree the way forward with my manager.'

    Once you have completed this technique for all of the activities on your *don't enjoy* list you can make your decision whether to include them in your ideal day (in their new *enjoyable* form) or whether you are going to stop them. You may find it helps to turn back to your original ideal day list and add any new activities to it. In order to truly achieve the right balance for *you*, you should not be doing any activities you don't enjoy. You may find that it takes some time to eliminate the unenjoyable ones, but we promise you your life will feel so much better once you've done it. You will wonder why you spent so much time doing things that you didn't enjoy.

Putting your ideal day into perspective

There is a very effective way of putting everything that is included in your ideal day into perspective. It is a written statement – an affirmation – of how much time you have each day to fit in everything you do. It is this:

> *There are 24 hours in a day. On average I get up at (7.30 a.m.) and go to bed at (11.30 p.m.). This gives me (16 hours) to fit in all my activities. This is enough time.*

Write this down now. Replace the figures in brackets with your own.

If this doesn't give you enough time go back and review your ideal day. You cannot have an ideal day in which it is not possible to fit in all the activities you have listed! As many of you will know from your own – or other's – experience, trying to do too much in a day can lead to stress and illness.

To complete this exercise, take a few moments to look back at the answers you gave to the questions in Chapter 1, particularly questions 3 *Where are you now?* and 4 *What do you want out of life?* Are the lists you have made above consistent with what you wrote down in the first chapter?

Remember to repeat this exercise to cover your ideal day when you are not working, e.g. at a weekend. Only by doing this will you be in a position to achieve the balance that is right for your life.

Exploring your values

Now you have had time to consider and write down the activities which you would like to make up your ideal day it is time to move a step further towards having a better life.

In Chapter 1 we asked you *How much quality time are you spending in the areas of your life that you value the most?* Turn back to page 7 to see how you answered this question. The following exercise (illustrated in Figure 7) will help you to focus on the different areas of your life that are important to you and whether the time you spend in these areas is in keeping with your own values.

In it you will need to categorise your life under four main headings:

◆ Work.

◆ Home/family.

◆ Health/leisure.

◆ Sleep.

You will need to think about and write down the order in which you value these areas of your life. You also need to work out whether the time you spend in each of these areas is consistent with the value you attribute to it. You will probably need to use a calculator for this exercise.

Instructions for completing your values table

1. *Order in which I value the areas of my life.*

Write down the order in which you value these areas of your life. The area you value most should be number '1', the next most important number '2', etc.

Sleep is included because it is something everyone needs and must have. However, for the purpose of this exercise you do not need to rank it against the other areas of your life.

2. *How my time is currently divided between these areas of my life.*

Work out the number of hours *in an average month* that you currently spend in each of these areas of your life.

For the purpose of this exercise an average month is 31 days or 744 hours – this includes four weekends (8 days or 192 hours).

Check to make sure the hours you have written down add up to 744.

3. Comments

Once you have filled in all the other details, write down any thoughts you have about the balance between the different areas of your life. Are you spending as much time as you would like in each area – or perhaps too much time?

This exercise will help you to focus your attention on how *in balance* or *out of balance* your life and your values are compared to how you would like them to be. You may find it interesting to return to this in a few months time and rework the figures after making adjustments to your life.

Figure 7 shows the *before* and *after* figures for someone whose life changed dramatically as a result of doing this exercise.

The case study on page 184 explains how it was possible to make such dramatic changes.

AREAS OF MY LIFE	ORDER IN WHICH I VALUE THESE AREAS OF MY LIFE	HOW MY TIME IS CURRENTLY DIVIDED BETWEEN THESE AREAS OF MY LIFE (HOURS)	COMMENTS
WORK	Before: 3 After: 2	Before: 386 After: 220	
HOME/ FAMILY	Before: 1 After: 1	Before: 100 After: 236	
HEALTH/ LEISURE	Before: 2 After 3:	Before: 10 After: 40	
SLEEP		Before: 248 After: 248	

Fig. 7. Example of a completed values table.

Case Study _____

'After working out the *before* set of figures it worried me to see how much of my time was spent at work and how little at home or on leisure. I was unhappy with my job and feeling very stressed at the time – little wonder when you look at the balance of hours! – My job involved travelling all over the country and I regularly left home on a Sunday afternoon and spent hours travelling to wherever I needed to be on the Monday morning. At the end of the week, I often didn't get home until the early hours of Saturday morning. In addition to all this I regularly brought work home with me. My home life was dismal although I had listed it as number '1' in my values I certainly wasn't spending very much quality time there. I knew something had to change.

I took a very dramatic step. I resigned from my high-status, highly paid job, giving up all the perks that went with it – a company car, a fuel card, a cheap-rate mortgage, an excellent pension scheme, six months sick pay if I was ill – and became self-employed. I did the same sort of work as before, only now I was doing it because I *wanted* to. I spent more time working from home. When I travelled I actually enjoyed it because I would listen to some nice music or take time to stop and look around at the scenery. It didn't feel like work and I didn't classify it as work. I made a conscious effort to put time aside for reading, walking, cooking a nice meal in the evening. The whole quality of my life improved in a very short space of time. But it took the above *values* exercise to crystallise where my life was *out of balance*. _____

Try it now   Now it's time for you to have a go at completing your own values table. Copy the grid into your notebook and fill in your own figures. Do this before reading any further.

How to get the greatest benefit from your values table

How does your values table look? Are you surprised by any of the figures? Do any adjustments need to be made to your life? If so, can you see where? Or perhaps you are happy with the figures. If you are that's great, because it confirms that you are already spending the *right* (i.e. right for you) amounts of time in those areas of your life where you want to spend them. However, even if you have got the *time* balance right, you may not have the *activity* balance right. In other words you might be spending the right amount of time at work, home, etc, but not necessarily doing things you enjoy. You will know whether the activity balance is right from the *ideal day* exercise that you completed earlier.

An important outcome of the *values* exercise should be to see if your values are in line with the time you spend in the different areas of your life. For example, maybe you value your home and family as number '1' but spend a lot less time there than at work. If this is the case you need to ask yourself if you have listed your values in the correct order. The answer will either be:

> 'Yes that is correct. My home and family are the most important things to me, but I accept that for us to have the lifestyle we want I need to spend more time at work than at home and I am happy to do that.'

Or

> 'I realise now that my work is the most important thing in my life at the moment. Without it I would not enjoy my life as much, nor would I be able to give my family all the good things we have. This doesn't mean I don't love my family very much – I do – but my work at the moment is the most important thing in my life.'

Or

> 'I realise now that I am spending far too much time at work. My family are far more important to me and I need to find a way to work this out.'

If you are not happy with any of the figures in your table what are you going to do about it?

Have you made some notes in the comments boxes? Remember it's up to you to make the changes you want – are you prepared to do this? If not are you prepared to accept that your life will carry on as it is now until you do something about it?

Again, refer back to the work you did in chapter one. Does your *values* table reflect what you said in chapter one? Refer also to your *ideal day* earlier in this chapter. Are your values consistent with the activities in your ideal day?

Once you are happy that all of these exercises are in

harmony with each other – in other words they are not giving conflicting messages – you are ready to move on to plan *how* to achieve what you want in your life.

Summary

In this chapter you have reached the point where you are ready to write the plan for building a better life. The exercises you have done to help you reach this point focused on:

◆ Your ideal day.
◆ Your values.

CHAPTER 11

Choosing a Better Life

I n this chapter you will find out how to set goals to help you on your journey towards a better life. Although it is the final chapter in the book, it should be the start of a happier, more fulfilled life in which you achieve the balance that is right for *your* life becoming more confident, more assertive, more motivated, better at communicating with other people, a positive thinker and a confident decision-maker.

> By understanding the power of loving, and valuing yourself, you can move forward without the emotional baggage which may have held you back in the past.

Setting goals

'No one can predict to what heights you can soar. Even you will not know until you spread your wings.'

Realising your dreams and achieving your goals can take a lot of hard work, some goals can take years to achieve. The work you do now, at the outset, when setting your goals will begin to pay dividends very quickly if you take the time to do it thoroughly.

Many of you reading this book will be familiar with the process of setting goals but how many of you have experienced the true *power* of setting goals *effectively*. There are enormous benefits to be gained from setting goals effectively – and conversely there are disadvantages in setting goals ineffectively. Below are just some of the benefits and disadvantages:

Benefits of setting goals effectively

◆ Achievable
◆ Motivating

- Clear and specific
- Positive effect

Disadvantages of setting goals ineffectively

- Unachievable
- Demotivating
- Unclear and vague
- Negative effect

This chapter will take you step by step through a process for setting goals effectively, and thus helping you to achieve what you want in your life.

If you speak to almost any successful person, or read books written by people who enjoy success and happiness both in their business and personal lives, they will acknowledge the power of setting goals. They believe, and have proved, that if you set realistic and challenging goals you can achieve them. Failure is a word you will rarely, if ever, hear in the vocabularies of such people. There is no such thing to them as failure, only flexibility, learning from their mistakes, and finding a more effective way to achieve their goals.

> If you speak to almost any successful person, they will acknowledge the power of setting goals.

No goals, no direction

If you never set goals, or if you set goals ineffectively, you are not likely to achieve them, and sadly life can become a wasteland of missed opportunities. How often do you hear people bemoaning the fact that they're bored with their job or their life, that other people have got better jobs and lifestyles than they have, etc? We come across many such people, and yet if we ask them what their goals in life are, more often than not they do not have any – or if they do they are expressed in such a way that they are unlikely ever to achieve them. A classic symptom of someone who says they are unhappy or unsuccessful is that they have no real goals, no purpose or direction in life. As a result they suffer a wide range of negative emotions – jealousy, envy, guilt, lack of confidence, low self-esteem, dissatisfaction, demotivation, unhappiness... This in turn results in them displaying many of the anti-influential behaviours that you looked at in chapter three. The great danger of having no direction, of lacking vision, is that rather than being in the driving seat of your life you can only react to the things and changes that other people impose on you. You end up living someone else's life script, not your own.

Goals versus dreams

Have you ever found yourself thinking, or saying, 'That's my dream house/car/job/holiday...?' Have you found yourself leafing through the pages of holiday brochures and dreaming of an all-inclusive fortnight in the Seychelles or the Caribbean? Or slavering over the beautiful houses in the estate agent's window or in *Country Life* magazine. Or covetously admiring the gleaming open-top sports car in the exclusive car showroom? Or imagining yourself earning thousands of pounds to give you the lifestyle you want?

An important distinction to be aware of is the difference between dreams and goals:

◆ a dream is *a series of pictures or events in the mind...a day-dream, fantasy: an ideal (i.e. existing only in idea).*
◆ a goal is *the object of a person's ambition or effort: a destination: an aim.*

(*Reader's Digest Oxford Dictionary*)

Can you see the difference? A *dream* tends to imply something in the realms of fantasy and which thus only happens in your mind or when you are asleep, whereas a *goal* implies something real and concrete. There is nothing wrong with having a dream, but bear in mind the fantasy element, and the potential impact this may have on your subconscious mind. If your subconscious mind believes something is *only a dream* it may well prevent you from believing that it can ever be real. If you *really* want that house, or car, or job, or holiday...then you must take steps to get it.

> Setting goals is the tool that has the power to turn your dreams into reality.

Setting goals effectively

Goal setting is only a useful tool if your goals are set effectively, in a way that will help you to achieve them. When setting goals there are some important points to bear in mind. Some may seem fairly obvious or minor, but it is amazing how many people fail to observe them and as a result fail to achieve their goals.

1. Know what you really want

This may sound very obvious, yet when you study it in more detail you will understand just how important it is to get this bit right! It is vital to check out the goal that you *think* you want before you try to achieve it. This involves being totally honest with yourself and continually asking yourself questions to test the validity of your goal. Play *devil's advocate* until you are sure you have set your true goal. Look at the following example to see how to do this:

A: *'One of my goals is to retire by the time I reach age 50.'*
B: *'Okay – why?'*
A: *'Well, I'd like to have more time to myself and to spend with my family.'*
B: *'Why?'*
A: *'I don't see much of them now because of my work.'*
B: *'So what would you do if you didn't have to go to work any more?'*
A: *'Go out more, play golf, relax at home, go shopping, go on more holidays...'*
B: *'How would you pay for all that?'*
A: *'With the money I'd saved up!'*
B: *'How much money would you need to save up to be able to sustain that lifestyle for you and your family – 50 is not old so you'd need some form of income for quite a few years.'*
A: *'I'm not sure.'*
B: *'Okay, well first work out how much money you'd need,*

and then whether it's possible to save that much before you reach 50.'

A: 'I can see that now.'

B: 'Do you think you'd be bored if you gave up work at 50?'

A: 'I can't wait to give up work.'

B: 'Is it work in general that you don't like, or is it the job you've got at the moment?'

A: 'I don't enjoy my job much at the moment.'

B: 'So if you changed your job to one you enjoyed, would you still want to give up work at 50?'

A: 'I'm not sure.'

B: 'What sort of work would you really like to do?'

A: 'I'd like to . . .'

B: 'If you could find that sort of work do you think you'd still want to retire at 50?'

A: 'Probably not.'

B: 'So is your goal to retire at 50 or to find a different job – one that you will enjoy doing?'

A: 'I'm not sure.'

B: 'Okay, let's look at it another way – if you carry on doing your current job, will you be able to afford to retire at 50?'

A: 'No.'

B: 'So you'd have to find another job anyway.'

A: 'Yes.'

B: 'If you found another job – one that you enjoyed – would you be able to afford to retire at 50?'

A: 'That would depend on how much I earned.'

B: 'Yes it would, but you've already said you'd like to work as a . . . Would that give you enough money between now and age 50?'

A: 'No, I doubt it.'

B: 'Okay, so once again let me ask you do you really believe that your goal is to retire at 50 or is it to find work you'll enjoy? Bear in mind the stress it might cause trying to save enough money to retire at 50.'

A: 'I guess what I really want is to find work I'll enjoy – it's not realistic to think I could afford to retire at 50, unless I could get a job that paid me a huge salary.'

B: 'Could you?'

A: 'Not with my present qualifications.'

B: *'So are you prepared to train for something else.'*

A: *'No, I don't really want to. I enjoy the type of work I do at the moment – I just don't enjoy my current job.'*

B: *'So what you're really saying is that you want to change your job...'*

As you can see from the above example, this questioning process may result in setting a totally different goal. However, it is best to discover this at the outset because if the goal is not completely right in the first place, the drive and motivation needed to achieve it are unlikely to be there.

2. Be specific

Can you remember what was said in chapter one about being specific when expressing what you want to achieve? You were advised to avoid using phrases like *I want to be happy, I want to be successful* as these only express the *feelings* that result from achieving your goal – they are not the goal itself (turn back to this chapter and look at it again if you need to refresh your memory in more detail).

If a goal is not expressed in specific terms it is difficult, if not impossible, to achieve.

In fact it can be unclear whether you have achieved it or not. The following examples illustrate this point:

◆ Vague: *'I want to lose weight.'*
◆ Specific: *'I will weigh 10 stone by Christmas this year.'*

◆ Vague: *'I want to change my job.'*
◆ Specific: *'I will set up my own business selling and repairing bicycles by 1 March next year.'*

◆ Vague: *'I want to be happy.'*
◆ Specific: list all the things you need to have or achieve to make you happy, e.g. *'I will have £20,000 in savings before I am 30', 'I will have two holidays abroad every year'* etc.

Specific goals contain a precise statement of what you want to achieve and when.

Because of this they are far more likely to be achieved as they leave little room for doubt or interpretation about what you are are aiming for.

3. *Express your goals in positive language*

The *specific* goals in the examples above all follow another important rule for effective goal setting: they are expressed in *positive* language. *I will...* is far more powerful than *I want to...*' The latter can imply an element of uncertainty about whether or not you will actually do it. *I* want *to travel around Australia for four months* but...

> Always strive to make your goals an expression of what you *do* want, not what you *don't*.

The example on the previous page illustrates this. By saying *I want to change my job* you are focusing your attention on the thing that you *don't* want – the job you're doing at the moment – rather than specifying what you *do* want – to set up my own business selling and repairing bicycles.

Yes, acknowledging that you want to change something is the *first step* to making the change, but when you are setting goals you must know what you want otherwise you cannot put all your energy into pursuing it and thus you may never know the joy of achieving it! Whenever there is even a hint of negativity or something that you *don't* want mentioned in the goal, it is the very thing your mind tends to focus on either consciously or subconsciously – and this can hinder you from achieving the goal. There has been much research carried out on this topic, particularly in the field of Neuro Linguistic Programming, which advocates the power of positive language. We have listed some books on this subject in the Further Reading section at the back of this book if you wish to study it further.

4. *Make sure your goal is SMART*

SMART is an acronym which stands for: Specific, Measurable, Achievable, Realistic and within a set Timsescale. Effective goals need to meet all of these criteria. Let's look at this in more detail:

Specific: We cannot stress enough the importance of making your goals specific. We have already discussed this above.

Measurable: To be effective your goal should be expressed in such a way that its result or outcome can be *measured* – this acts as proof that you have achieved it! In other words, whenever possible it should have a quantifiable or tangible target to aim for. For example, if you goal is *to run a mile in five minutes*, you can easily tell when you have achieved this goal because both the time and distance are measurable. But if you only state that you want to *improve your running speed* there is no specific measure to indicate when you have achieved this – there is nothing concrete to aim for.

Sometimes you will need to do some deep thinking in order to find a way to express your goal in measurable terms – but if you miss out this criterion your goal will be less effective.

Achievable: Goals need to be challenging and motivating in order to stimulate you, but they should not be so challenging that they are virtually impossible to achieve. For example, if you are fifty pounds overweight and extremely unfit it may not be a good idea to set yourself a goal of running the London marathon in one month's time! Theoretically the goal is achievable, but you stand a much better chance of achieving it if you set yourself a target to run it next year, giving yourself much more time to prepare.

> If a goal is achievable it also needs to be within your control.

Remember what we said earlier in the book about setting goals that involve other people or things that are not within your control – this can prove very frustrating.

Realistic: This goes hand in hand with *achievable* – if you set goals that are unrealistic then they are likely to be unachievable too – and what is more they can be stressful and demotivating. A realistic goal is one that you know is within your power to achieve, albeit you may need to put in a lot of time and effort. Climbing Mount Everest is only a realistic goal if you are prepared to go through all the arduous training that is needed to prepare yourself for such a task.

Timescale: It is important to state *when* you will achieve your goal in order to give you a target date to aim for. Some goals are very large, or long-term and if this is the case it is often more motivating to break them down into a series of sub-goals, each with its own target date.

The great danger of not setting a timescale is that your goal will drift and you may start to make excuses to delay achieving it.

Below are some examples of putting goals to the SMART test.

Goal = I want to lose weight

Specific: No. To be effective it must specify your target weight.

Measurable: Yes, but because the *Specific* criteria above was not effective you would meet this criteria if you lost just one ounce!

Achievable: Yes, because it is within your control, but the same comments apply as above.

Realistic: As above.

Timescale: No. There is no date specified by which you will achieve your goal therefore some of the motivation to achieve it is likely to be lacking. By not setting a timescale it can encourage you to procrastinate!

Goal = I want to be successful

Specific: No. To be effective it needs to define exactly what success means to you. This may result in several goals rather than just one.

Measurable: No – because it is not specific enough there is nothing to measure!

Achievable: You will not know the answer to this until you define *successful*.

Realistic: As above.

Timescale: No. Because it is not specific you cannot put a timescale on it.

Goal = I will learn to speak basic Spanish before I go on holiday to Spain in July this year

Specific: Yes.

Measurable: Theoretically yes, but to be fully effective you need to go even further and define what you mean by *basic* Spanish and how you will know that you have achieved this standard – a certificate, an examination?

Achievable: Yes.

Realistic: Yes, provided you have enough time before July.

Timescale: Yes.

Goal = I will achieve an Open University degree in psychology by 31 December five years from now

Specific: Yes.

Measurable: Yes.

Achievable: Yes, provided you know you are academically capable.

Realistic: Yes, provided you are prepared to put in the time and effort – if five years is not enough time, set a more realistic date.

Timescale: Yes.

> Whenever you set yourself a goal, put it to the SMART test to check its effectiveness.

If your goal doesn't meet *any one* of the above criteria you will need to rethink it! Sometimes it is simply a case of re-wording the goal, but in other cases it will be necessary to completely rethink what it is that you are trying to achieve.

5. Break it down into bite-size chunks if necessary

Goals fall into three main categories: *short-term, medium-term* and *long-term*. Sometimes it is necessary to break a goal down into *bite-size chunks*, particularly if it is a very large or long-term goal. By setting a series of sub-goals it means that you are achieving success at various steps along the way rather than just at the end.

For example, when we started writing this book we set

ourselves an overall goal to have the first draft finished in six months. However, we found this goal to be somewhat daunting and overpowering – we found it difficult to motivate ourselves to start on such a seemingly huge task. So we set a series of sub-goals – we would write the first chapter by a certain date and so on. This was far more motivating and it also seemed to make the task far easier and more enjoyable because it gave us a sense of achievement each time we achieved a sub-goal. Had we not set these sub-goals we may still have been struggling to start! As it is, we achieved our goal within five days of the target date.

You'd be surprised how many people fail to achieve their goals because they are unattainable and yet they do not think to break them down into more manageable chunks. This is particularly important if the goal you are setting is a long-term or medium-term goal – it helps enormously to experience a feeling of success along the way in order to motivate you to continue. If you have been courageous enough to set yourself medium-term and long-term goals surely you deserve to experience a growing sense of achievement along the way? By setting short(er) term sub-goals you can do this.

6. Are you prepared to do what is necessary to achieve your goal?

Some goals will be easier to achieve than others. We have already looked at the importance of making goals challenging but at the same time achievable and realistic. We need to emphasise a word of caution here about setting goals that are *too easy* to achieve. Although this may give you an initial sense of euphoria there will not be a very great or lasting sense of achievement when you reach such goals!

> By all means have one or two *easy* goals if this helps to motivate you, but make sure that the majority are challenging.

This part of the goal-setting process involves being totally honest with yourself, as in point 1 above. You need to ask yourself *what do I need to do/know/have/sacrifice in order to achieve my goal?* Then ask yourself if you are prepared to pay this price. If you are not, change your goal – modify it or change it altogether.

7. Keep the number of goals manageable

The idea of setting goals and writing them down is to help you achieve them. On average we (Frank and Hilary, the authors of this book) each set between 10–15 goals which we hope to achieve *within* the year. Some goals relate to our business, some are personal, all of them are SMART! We also have 20–30 longer term goals, some extending well into the future.

We found that our goals were much more effective when we spent quality time working on them and writing them down. Initially this took us a whole day, but the results were worth it. Our goals met all the SMART criteria, and we found that we achieved them with astonishing regularity. This made an amazing difference to the quality of both our lives, and the lives of our families. We cannot emphasise enough the power of setting effective goals.

> Always try to keep the number of goals manageable.

It can be very demotivating to have too many goals because they can take a long time to achieve – if you achieve them at all. Having a reasonable number of attainable, but challenging goals is far more motivating.

8. Write it down

Again this may sound obvious, but writing a goal down can have a tremendous impact on whether or not you achieve it.

In a study carried out at Yale University in 1953 students were asked if they had specific, written down goals and plans for achieving them. Only 3 per cent had such goals. Twenty years later, the researchers interviewed all of the surviving members of the 1953 class. They discovered that the 3 per cent with specific, written down goals were worth more in financial terms than all of the others put together and enjoyed high levels of happiness.

A more recent American study showed that 90 per cent of people who write down their goals achieve them.

Writing the goal down is symbolic of making a commitment. A goal that is not written down is easy to avoid. Think about the difference between a written contract and a verbal one – which do you feel more comfortable with, and why? The chances are it's the written one because it provides a stronger sense of commitment. The same applies to goals.

Setting your own goals

The following exercise is one of the most important in the book and can provide the impetus to move you towards a better life.

Keeping in mind all of the things you have learned throughout this book, and all the previous exercises you have done, you are now ready to set your goals effectively. Even if you have already set goals, now is the time to review them in the light of what you have learned and to put them to the SMART test to see if they are as effective as they could be.

In setting your goals you will need to refer to the work you did in chapters nine and ten – and indeed throughout the book. Make sure you set goals to cover:

◆ All the areas of your life you want to change.

◆ All the things you want to achieve or have.

> The combination of these goals is your ticket to a better life.

This is an exercise that should be treated with respect and given plenty of time to complete – you may not be able to do it all in one go. First let's summarise the eight criteria for setting goals effectively:

1. Know what you really want.

2. Be specific.

3. Express your goals in positive language.

4. Make sure your goal is SMART.

5. Break it down into *bite-size chunks* if necessary.

6. Are you prepared to do what is necessary to achieve your goal?

7. Keep the number of goals manageable.

8. Write it down.

Try it now   In your notebook write down your *short-term, medium-term* and *long-term* goals. You may prefer to use a separate page for each heading so that you can add to it at will.

Achieving your goals

Having set your goals you need to give some careful consideration to planning how you are going to achieve them. You may have partly done this by setting sub-goals – steps along the way. But have you really thought about what it's going to take to achieve your goals, the physical and mental effort you will need to put in?

Ask yourself the following question in relation to each of the goals you have set: *What can I do today (or this week/ month/year) to help me achieve this goal?*

In other words, what steps can you take *now* to move towards your goal? Does what you need to do fit in with your ideal day and your values? If not, why not? Perhaps you need to revise one of these areas – your ideal day, your values, or your goals. To have a better life, *all* of these areas must be compatible.

Some people find it very useful and motivating to write a *to do* list, with all the things they are going to do during the day or week or month to help achieve their goals. This is like setting mini-goals and can be motivating when you tick them off.

Alternatively you may like to make a *to do* list for each of your goals, breaking it down into all the things you need to do to achieve it. Part of this may simply involve finding out more information: *How much is my holiday to the Seychelles going to cost? Where do I want to stay? What can I do when I get there – what is there to see? How expensive is the cost of living? What sort of food do they eat? What's the best time of year to go there? etc.* The more you can break your goal down, the more real it will seem. You will often find yourself so deeply involved in it that you actually feel as though you have already achieved it! That's great, the clearer your picture of what it will be like, and the stronger your emotions, then the more motivated you should feel.

You may find it inspires and motivates you to have a picture of some of your goals – a car, a holiday destination, a house... – where you can look at them often. Perhaps frame them and hang them in the lounge, the dining room, the kitchen, or the bedroom.

Try it now	For each of your goals, analyse very carefully all the things you will need to do in order to achieve it. Write these things down in your notebook in a way that you will find them motivating, for example a daily *to do* list. You may like to include pictures of your goal if appropriate.

Reviewing your goals and monitoring progress

Once you have set your goals and worked out how you are going to achieve them, you need to review them on a regular basis. This includes doing all of the following if appropriate:

◆ Tick off your goals as you achieve them.
◆ Check that you are still on line to achieve your remaining goals.
◆ Add any new goals that you would like to achieve.
◆ Delete any goals you no longer wish to achieve.
◆ Amend any goals you need to change.
◆ Amend the timescale for achieving any goals if you need to.

> It is far better to amend your goals rather than struggle to achieve them.

Never think that you have failed just because you do not achieve all of your goals in the original timescales. Accept that sometimes circumstances will mean you need to make changes. Indeed, many people find that as they achieve their shorter term goals, their longer term goals no longer represent what they want in life anyway. If this is the case, the sooner you amend your goals the sooner you can begin to work towards your new ones.

Let's use our own experience to show you how goals can be

adjusted. As we said earlier when we originally decided to write this book we wanted to complete it within six months.

However, shortly after setting this goal we were offered a large training contract which involved running the course on which the book is based. We sat down straight away to review our goals. We knew that we could not do both things effectively, so we decided to put the book on hold for 12 months, and moved our goal back accordingly. By doing this we earned enough money to enable us to take some time off later to write the book. It's difficult to explain how good it felt – achieving a goal is something very personal, and each person reacts differently to it. But let's just say it felt very good and it made all the hard work worthwhile.

So, don't worry too much if outside influences prevent you from achieving your original set of goals. Review them, revise them, and set out to achieve the new goals with a renewed vigour. You should only begin to worry if your goals are proving demotivating, or if you regularly fail to achieve them. If this is the case, read back over the earlier information in this chapter on setting effective goals and see where you are going wrong.

Summary

When you put this book down, having finished, and we hope enjoyed it, your life will carry on. The day-to-day issues you face will still be there – people and relationships to deal with, problems to sort out. The intention of this book is to help you handle these situations effectively. We hope you will use it for continual reference.

You are now acquiring the tools to help you choose a better life. You have looked at how to put the past into perspective and how to set effective goals that move you towards the life you want. You have also learned how to love and value yourself and be more assertive. As you worked through the *Try it now* exercises you should have felt your confidence and self-esteem growing until, having reached the end, you have a clearer picture of what you must do to build a new future.

This book is dedicated to helping people grow and have a happy and fulfilled life. We sincerely hope it has helped *you*.

Further Reading

Feel the Fear and Do It Anyway, Susan Jeffers (Rider)

Putting Assertiveness to Work, Graham Willcocks and Steve Morris (Pitman Publishing)

Even Eagles Need a Push, David McNally (Thorsons)

The Seven Habits of Highly Effective People, Stephen R Covey (Simon and Schuster)

NLP: The New Art and Science of Getting What You Want, Dr Harry Alder (Piatkus)

Think and Grow Rich, Napoleon Hill (Wilshire Book Company)

The Road Less Travelled, M Scott Peck (Simon and Schuster)

Index